10⁰⁰

AIR COMBAT COMMAND

Global Power for America

The United State Air Force's

AIR COMBAT COMMAND

Global Power for America

by Randy Jolly

with William D. Mason

TABLE OF CONTENTS

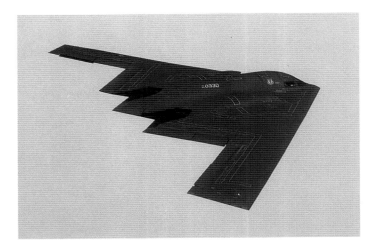

INTRODUCTION 5

8TH AIR FORCE

2d Bomb Wing, Barksdale AFB 6
5th Bomb Wing, Minot AFB 12
7th Bomb Wing, Dyess AFB 26
27th Fighter Wing, Cannon AFB 38
28th Bomb Wing, Ellsworth AFB 46
314th Airlift Wing, Little Rock AFB 56
509th Bomb Wing, Whiteman AFB 70

9TH AIR FORCE

1st Fighter Wing, Langley AFB 80
4th Wing, Seymour Johnson AFB 88
20th Fighter Wing, Shaw AFB 102
23d Wing, Pope AFB 116
33d Fighter Wing, Eglin AFB 130
347th Wing, Moody AFB 140

12TH AIR FORCE

9th Reconnaissance Wing, Beale AFB 148
49th Fighter Wing, Holloman AFB 156
55th Wing, Offutt AFB 164
355th Wing, Davis-Monthan AFB 168
366th Wing, Mountain Home AFB 180
388th Fighter Wing, Hill AFB 200
552nd Air Control Wing, Tinker AFB 208

U.S. AIR FORCE FIGHTER WEAPONS SCHOOL 211

JOINT STARS 218

F-22 222

ACKNOWLEDGEMENTS 224

International Standard Book Number 0-9624862-9-9
Library of Congress Catalog Number 95-76000
© All photos copyright Randy Jolly 1995 except where noted
Published by: Aero Graphics Inc.
4729 Lawler Road – Garland, Texas 75042-4506
214-276-2544 FAX: 214-276-5494
Designer – Laurie Adams
Printed in Hong Kong through Bookbuilders Ltd.

America cannot afford to be the second place finisher in any conflict. The world's sole remaining super power must always be the one there, "the furstest with the mostest." While that phrase was coined during the Civil War, it was never more true than today. The next threat to freedom that this country faces probably will not be as accommodating as the Iraqis, allowing us and our coalition allies six months to position our forces, coordinate our strategy and pick our targets. The next threat we face will more likely develop within a matter of days rather than months, and force our military to be ready to swing into action immediately.

Fortunately, this fact has been recognized by our military leaders and our forces are being shaped to meet these challenges. In the Air Force, Air Combat Command has been formed to be America's quick reaction strike force, ready to deploy and employ air power decisively, wherever it may be needed, at whatever level of intensity is required. Formed in June of 1992 from the assets of the Strategic and Tactical Air Commands, Air Combat Command, (or ACC), has forged a powerful, well trained and equipped force, despite the pressures of downsizing and budgetary constraints. Combining the strengths inherent in the two organizations it absorbed with new concepts, such as composite wings, ACC stands ready to project air power to any corner of the globe at a moments notice. The command's capabilities are borne on the wings of an impressive array of aircraft. From 30 plus year old B-52s, U-2s and KC-135s to fresh-off-the-assembly-line F-16s, F-15Es and B-2s, ACC's 3,400 aircraft are well prepared to put "fire and steel" on the target.

For the first time, the Air Force has placed in one command all the "stuff" required to prosecute a conflict at all levels. But what makes ACC truly a force to be reckoned with is not the "stuff" but the people. Over 174,000 people, who, from single-stripe airmen to four star generals share a common bond of professionalism and performance that makes Air Combat

Command the standard by which all other air forces are measured. Whether they're fighter pilots, maintainers or motor pool dispatchers, ACC's people and their dedication are what ensure the success of the command's mission.

That mission is carried out at bases through-out the world. Because of the nature of their work, ACC people are "on the road" constantly - the average aircrew member in the 552nd AWACS Wing at Tinker, for instance, is away from home more than 200 days a year. Their compatriots in bomber, fighter, reconnaissance and airlift units are not far behind. So while all the pictures in this book were shot in the United States, remember that the background of these photos could just as well have been the sands of the Middle East or the jungles of Central America. This book is an attempt to show what goes on routinely at bases through-out the command. It is a snapshot, both literally and figuratively, of training flights and aircraft maintenance. Unfortunately, what this overview cannot show, in the space available, are the thousands of support troops without whom not a sortie would be flown or a wrench turned. You might not see them in the pictures, but they are there. We hope that in the words and pictures that follow that we have captured the essence of the world's premier air combat force - Air Combat Command, because to us they are truly Real Heroes.

Barksdale Air Force Base, Louisiana, might well be called "Bombertown, USA". It houses Headquarters, Eighth Air Force which controls almost all of Air Combat Command's bomber assets and is also the home of 49 B-52s assigned to the 2nd Bomb Wing and it's 11th, 20th and 96th Bomb Squadrons, as well as the only Air Force Reserve B-52 squadron, the 93rd. All of these units stand ready to carry out the B-52's original mission - nuclear strike - but today expect to be called on to carry conventional weapons, perhaps half-way round the globe, as the front line of American deterrence and power projection.

Seen here are the rituals that the crew goes through prior to each and every mission whether it's a local training hop or taking the fight to the enemy in combat half a world away. The crew comes in to the squadron to brief the sortie three to four hours prior to takeoff (top). Every aspect of the mission is covered in detail, then about an hour prior to takeoff, they board the crew bus. After a stop at wing life support, to pick up helmets, and survival gear, it's out to the jet. Here they are met by the aircraft's crew chief, who briefs them on the maintenance status of the plane. (middle). Then it's just a matter of the 5 person crew running through 45 minutes worth of checklists (bottom and left) before the BUFF is ready to taxi for takeoff.

The capability of the B-52 to strike targets from the United States has also been shown during wartime. Some of the first weapons to strike Iraq during DESERT STORM were AGM-86C Conventional Air Launched Cruise Missiles (CALCM) launched from seven B-52s. These BUFFs had taken off from Barksdale and after a 7,000 mile flight fired 35 CALCMs which struck priority, highly defended targets through-out Iraq. Their missions successfully com-

pleted, the B-52s returned to Barksdale finishing the longest combat missions in history: 35 hour, 14,000 mile sorties.

These missions didn't max-out the B-52's capabilities. The BUFF can carry nearly 70,000 pounds of ordinance, including up to 20 CALCM. Such a load is seen here being uploaded by munitions specialists of the 2nd Bomb Wing. Wing pylons have CALCMs pre-loaded at the munitions storage area and then brought to the aircraft on a MHU-196 trailer. The trailer is wheeled into posi-

tion underneath the BUFF's wings and the pylon raised and attached.

Eight more rounds are loaded on a common strategic rotary launcher or CSRL which munitions troops are shown sliding into place in the bomb bay. In addition to CALCMs, the BUFF can also carry up to 51 MK-82/84/M117 iron bombs, or, 26 MK-41 2000 lb sea mines, or 8 AGM-84 Harpoon anti-shipping missiles or 4 AGM-142 Have Nap glide bombs.

B-52 crews have repeatedly demonstrated their ability to carry out their "global power" mission, most recently in August 1994. During an exercise two B-52H aircraft with a total of 16 aircrew of the 96th Bomb Squadron took off from Barksdale, flew to a range in Kuwait, attacked a simulated target and continued on to circumnavigate the globe. The target was attacked with 54 MK82 500-lb bombs which were dropped within 3 seconds of the scheduled time, this after flying 20 hours. 27 hours later, after a 20,000 mile non-stop flight, the two B-52s landed at Barksdale with fewer than a dozen write-ups (maintenance problems). Outstanding testimony to the capabilities of the jets, their crews - and the folks who maintain these 30 year old machines.

Opposite page:
A 96th Bomb Squadron B-52H on low approach over Barksdale. The 96th is responsible for training all Air Force B-52 crews.

This page:
A B-52H of the 93rd Bomb Squadron, the only Air Force Reserve squadron to fly the venerable BUFF.

Previous page:
Straining to haul 488,000 pounds aloft, a B-52H of the 5th Bomb Wing takes-off from Minot AFB, ND on a typical "cold" winter morning on the northern tier.

Opposite page:
Blistering hot or freezing cold, in rain, snow, sunshine or fog, the crew chief has to hustle while launching his or her jet.

This page:
With the fire guard posted and the auxiliary power unit providing a much needed assist, 5th Bomb Wing B-52H starts engines at the beginning of another sortie. ALQ-172 ECM system antennas can be seen on fuselage sides, while the housings for the Electro-optical Viewing System sensors are underneath the nose.

While flightline maintainers launch, recover and turn jets, troops in the phase docks provide periodic, in-depth inspections. During "phase," every panel that can be removed is pulled, as a BUFF gets the equivalent of an annual check-up. Both the basic structure of the airplane and all the systems that go into it get a through examination, everything that can be checked - is. Here, personnel of the 5th MS inspect the TF-33P-3 engines of a B-52H while corrosion control is performed on a section of cowling. Corrosion control is a priority item on these 30 year old machines.

Capable of hauling 70,000 lbs of ordinance, B-52 get loaded with weapons by the truck load. Here, a partial load of MK-82 AIR 500lb bombs are loaded prior to a training sortie. The blue color of the bomb casing indicates they are inert - iron bomb casings filled with concrete instead of explosive. Dropping heavyweight inert ordinance is a valuable training event for both maintainers, who get to practice loading full-size and weight weapons and for aircrews, who get to experience the handling characteristics of a fully loaded airplane. Inert weapons are also

cheaper than live rounds and can be dropped on more ranges. The Air-Inflatable Retarder tail assembly on the bomb is basically a can with a fabric bag inside. Once clear of the jet after release, the bag is deployed, fills with air and drastically slows the bomb, allowing the B-52 to drop weapons at low altitude and still escape their effects. Without the additional drag of the AIR, the low drag MK-82 would detonate virtually underneath the delivery aircraft - not a morale enhancing tactic

Bombs are pulled off the trailer and transported individually to the jet by an MJ-1B, called a "jammer" by munitions personnel, it's a cross between a go-cart and a crane. Along with the bomb bay door, a portion of the side of the B-52 swings up to allow the jammer, and it's cargo, access to the bomb racks. Notice the removal of the tail gun and the not-so-aerodynamic closure of the ensuing gap.

Decision to remove the guns (and gunners) from all B-52s was an emotional one, but recognized the fact that B-52 would only be utilized in areas of complete air superiority.

Previous page:
B-52H, loaded with 24 MK-82 500 lb bombs, enroute to the range on a training exercise. AIR tail sections can be used for high-drag for low altitude deliveries or configured to come off "slick" for medium and high altitude deliveries.

This page:
B-52H of 23rd Bomb Squadron, cruises to the tanker track above typical North Dakota winter terrain. Even with a 6000 lbs/minute transfer rate, the BUFF can hang on the boom for up to 30 minutes replenishing its fuel supply.

Following page:
Refueling complete, the BUFF heads for the start point of a low-level route. Typical peacetime training sorties include a high level bomb run, air refueling, low-level work followed by returning to the "home-drome" for practice instrument approaches and landings – and take about 8 hours. Those eight flying hours are preceded by 4 to 6 hours of planning the day prior, 2 to 3 hours of pre-flight briefing and preparation the day of the flight and are followed by 2 to 3 hours of de-briefing. All of this is to ensure that the maximum amount of training is extracted from each flying hour.

It's as fast as a fighter, pilots say it handles like a fighter, but boy those chocks are a whole lot bigger than a fighter's. Crew chief hustles to get the chocks, and himself, out of the way as a "Bone" of the 9th Bomb Squadron starts to taxi at Dyess AFB, TX.

SAC authorized nose art on its aircraft as a matter of tradition; while ACC has not allowed this practice to spread to fighters, they have allowed it to continue on ex-SAC aircraft. The center example of nose art also illustrates the B-1's unofficial nickname. In an early article on the aircraft,

a clueless reporter referred to the "B ONE" throughout the story, aircrews almost universally now call the jet the "Bone".

The 9th is one of four squadrons assigned to the 7th Wing. The 7th is a combined wing - a unit that has different types of aircraft assigned but that does

not expect to be deployed or fight together. In this case B-1s of the 9th and 28th Bomb Squadrons are combined with C-130s of the 39th and 40th Airlift Squadrons. While the 9th is an operational unit, the 28th has a dual tasking. In addition to meeting operational taskings, it also is

the B-1 schoolhouse, training all B-1 crews for both active duty and National Guard units. Both the 39th and 40th are operational units, deploying aircraft, crews and maintainers worldwide to carry out their intra-theater airlift mission.

How do you put 84 Mk-82 500 lb bombs in a B-1? Very carefully! Munitions troops show how, during weapons load training. First, bombs are "built up" in the munitions storage area, combining the main body of the bomb with a tail section - in this case the Air Inflatable Retarder (AIR). The AIR tail section increases drag on the bomb after release, allowing low altitude attacks to be made. Then the built up

weapons are taken to the flightline on a flatbed truck for loading into an aircraft. An MHU-83 "jammer" (above) picks them up off the truck and inserts them in the bomb bay. A munitions troop must go up a ladder to guide the bomb's shackles into the ejector rack and lock them into place (left). He then "carts" the pylon - adding small explosive charges that open the suspension hooks and kick the bomb away from the pylon at

weapons release. Finally, he adds the fuse to the bomb and runs the arming wires from it to the pylon. Each bomb has two fuse wells, one in the nose and one in the tail. These bombs have nose plugs - solid steel plugs filling the nose fuse wells to aid in punching into hard targets. The AIR tail assembly has a small door in its side allowing access to the tail fuse well. A proficient crew can get a bomb off the truck, loaded and

armed up in under four minutes. B-1 suspension equipment is unique, using arms to hold the bombs. These fold down to lay against the right side of the bomb bay after releasing their weapons. Each bomb bay has two sets of three arms in tandem. At left you can see the top arm has been loaded, (fore and aft), the middle arm is being loaded (aft) and the bottom arms are folded down.

Previous page:
A 28th Bomb Squadron B-1B releases insert 500-lb bombs over Melrose Range in eastern New Mexico. "Bones" make extensive use of their long legs on training sorties, visiting ranges through-out the world.

This page:
All bomber units in ACC now have T-38s assigned as a part of the Companion Training Program (CTP). This very popular program allows co-pilots, when not planning missions or flying their regular aircraft, to fly CTP aircraft to build hours and experience, improving their flying skills, judgment and situational aware ness. It's a win-win situation, ACC gets a more experienced aircrew member, faster (and cheaper) and the co-pilots get to fly more. A minimum of 15 sorties per quarter are required. Dyess T-38s, assigned to the 9th Bomb Squadron, are camouflaged and marked identically to the squadron's B-1s.

Facing page:
As a B-1 waits "number one" for takeoff, a string of 40th Airlift Squadron C-130s approach runway 34. With generally great flying weather year-round and its mid-continent location, Dyess attracts considerable transient traffic. Combined with the activities of the four resident flying squadrons, scenes such as this are common place.

Previous page:
With no self-defense armament, the B-1s standard
tactic when threatened is to
get real low, real fast.
Thicker air at low altitude
shrinks missile envelopes
and increases radar clutter,
complicating tracking the
aircraft. By terrain masking, getting down between
hills and ridge lines, radar
contact can be broken
while the B-1 makes a
hasty getaway. To practice
this, Dyess "Bones" make

extensive use of IR-178 in
southwest Texas. Here a
9th Bomb Squadron jet
scoots along at 600 feet
and 540 knots.

This page:
Dyess C-130s "live
deployed." In the past year
the 39th and 40th's 25 aircraft have been deployed to
support Operation Provide
Comfort in Turkey, Opera-
tion Uphold Democracy in
Haiti as well as spending
three months of the year in
Saudi Arabia as part of the

rotation shared with Pope
and Little Rock C-130
units. (Top right) Propul-
sion specialists have the
prop spinner off as they
work a write up. One of
the biggest problems in
deploying any "large air-
plane" unit is the amount
of airlift taken up moving
support equipment, like
the B-4 stand seen here.
C-130 units are self-
deployable, but other units
(B-1 and E-3 for example)
give up valuable C-141 and

C-5 space moving relatively light but bulky stands.
(Top left) Practicing touch
and go's, a 40th Herc
shows off its new camou-
flage scheme. While
bland, the all-over grey
scheme makes maintainers
work easier, (being easier
to apply), is logistically
simpler, (since there's only
one type of paint to stock)
and is more effective hid-
ing the airplane at
altitude.

Poor C² Communications Can Clip The Warrior's Wings

INFORMATION FROM ANYWHERE, TO EVERYWHERE... ANYTIME

Rockwell's Communication Systems Division (CSD) delivers command and control communications (C²) to the airborne warrior when, where, and how he needs it. CSD expertise covers the entire frequency spectrum – from VLF through EHF – for theater, major regional conflicts, and global applications.

CSD designs, integrates, and implements secure and clear voice/data communications, data processing, message handling and switching, and information management requirements for airborne and mobile platforms, as well as fixed installations. CSD's line of stackable transit cases and shelterized multimedia communication and information handling systems are ideally suited to theater deployable applications requiring compactness, rapid mobility, operational flexibility, and ease of setup and operation.

CSD airborne systems provide C² information and support for global missions, special operations, tactical, and national security requirements.

Whether it be for broadcasting critical emergency action messages, pinpointing a target location, or helping maintain weapon or aircraft availability, Rockwell is instrumental in helping direct and deliver the steel to the target.

For further information contact:

Communication Systems Division
Rockwell International Corporation
3200 East Renner Road
Richardson, Texas 75082-2402
Phone 214.705.3950

 Rockwell Defense Electronics

Caption opposite page:
The size of the F-111 is evident as maintenance personnel work to fix a hydraulic problem. Maintainers rarely have the pleasure of working on their charges in the comfort of a hangar - problems are found and fixed in whatever conditions Mother Nature provides.

This page:
The F-111 is a labor intensive device when it comes to maintenance. Here, specialists pull a line replaceable unit in a process referred to as "swap-tronics" - Swap LRUs and if the problem is fixed, then the bad LRU is on its way to the shop for repair while the jet is ready for the next sortie. (If the problems not solved, then its time to swap-out another LRU.) Notice that the so-called black boxes are really grey.

Previous spread:
Maintainers swarm around a F-111F during the "last chance" inspection at the End Of the Runway prior to takeoff. In addition to pulling munition safety pins, EOR troops also inspect tires and check for leaks and loose panels. This F-111 is carrying two SUU-20 bomb dispensers which hold 6 BDU-33 practice bombs each, a typical load for a peacetime training mission bound for the bombing range.

Opposite page:
F-111E with 12 MK-82AIR bombs, on the way to Melrose range in Southeast New Mexico. ACC wants each of it's aircrew to drop "heavyweight" (full size vs sub-scale practice ordinance) at least once every six months. For those that do not have the opportunity to do this during Red Flag or at other large scale exercises, a limited number of sorties are available, flown from home station to a local range.

This page:
With the Pave Tack pod illuminating the target with laser energy, an F-111F of the 523 FS releases a GBU-10 over Melrose range. The 13.5 foot long Pave Tack pod normally is stowed in the weapons bay and is semi-extended only during an attack. The articulated ball of the Pave Tack, visible directly above the GBU-10's forward wings, contains an imaging infrared sensor to see/track the target and a coaxial laser that provides both range to the target (for weapons release computations) and target illumination (for weapon guidance after release).

Team Cannon - an EF-111 and a F-111E armed with MK-82 bombs maneuver over southern New Mexico. The EF-111 is the marriage of the F-111A airframe with the jamming package from the EA-6B; it provides standoff and escort jamming of threat radars for strike aircraft, essentially "putting the eyes out" of enemy air defense systems. The big advantage the EF-111 has over the EA-6B is speed, being able to keep up with penetrating strike aircraft, no matter how fast they go.

ENCORE PERFORMANCE.

Grumman did it before – developing the EF-111A's tactical jamming system to detect, identify and disrupt the enemy's electronic air defenses. Now we're doing it again on the Air Force's Systems Improvement Program. Testing is underway and as a proven system integrator with over 30 years of experience in electronic warfare, we know we can deliver a new system with increased performance, flexibility and reliability. And deliver it on time with the lowest risk.

The winning team: Northrop Grumman, ACA, AIL, Comptek, IBM and Smiths.

The Northrop Grumman Team

NORTHROP GRUMMAN

Previous page:
Steel rain - A B-1B of the 28th Bomb Wing, Ellsworth AFB, SD unleashes 27 MK-82 500 lb bombs from it's three bomb bays in a medium altitude attack. This represents only a fraction of it's total capacity - 84 MK-82s.

Opposite:
The "Bone" crew in it's element - at night, at low altitude and going fast. While much maligned in the media; the only critics who really know the jet, the aircrew, praise it highly. Typical comments include praises of the aircraft's handling and power plus the quality of it's radar and terrain following systems. Top photo - Aircraft commander and pilot. Lower photos - Offensive Systems Operator and Defensive Systems Operator.

This page:
What makes the B-1 unique among ACC bombers is speed. While other bombers are limited to subsonic velocities, the B-1 can keep up with anything the fighters in the strike package can hack. This tremendously simplifies the strikers job, not having to be tied down with a large, slow moving "Mig-Magnet". The package spends less time exposed to the threat and air-to-air escorts don't have to fly daisy-chains to match their 450kt + speeds to 300kt - bombers.

Maintainers of the 28th Bomb Wing work to prepare a B-1 for it's next sortie. Even after switching to the demanding conventional role, the B-1 continues to meet or exceed all ACC established goals for sortie generation and in-commission rates - due to efforts like this.

Opposite page:
B-1B crew chief prepares to launch his jet on another training sortie. While the B-1 retains the capability to start all four engines simultaneously, normally engines are cranked one at a time. The "Bone" requires no external support equipment for launch and recovery, greatly simplifying both deployment logistics and off-station operations.

B-1B in the radar pattern, sets up to fly a practice instrument approach at the end of another sortie. B-1's swing wing gives it the capability to take-off and land at 170 knots while flying an attack at 550 knots +. Wings sweep from 15 to 67.5 degrees, taking 53 seconds for full travel. Take-offs and landings are done at 15/20 degree settings, normal cruise is at 25 degrees, and attacks are made with the wings fully swept. Aircraft at left, being towed, shows-off nose art marking it as the high time aircraft in the B-1 fleet.

28th Bomb Wing B-1B over it's home station, Ellsworth AFB, SD. After landing, the crew gathers beneath the aircraft. B-1 is flown by a crew of four: Aircraft Commander, Pilot, Offensive Systems Operator and Defense Systems Operator. ACC is dual qualifying the OSOs and DSOs, allowing the crew greater flexibility during long sorties.

Following spread:
B-1B about to enter a low level route. The B-1's ter- rain following system allows the aircraft to pene- trate at altitudes from 200 to 2000 feet completely hands off while following the contours of the terrain exactly. This allows a lower, and thus more likely a surprise approach to the target, than older systems that have to use a terrain avoidance system and are forced to fly higher.

This page:
C-130E of the 314th Airlift
Wing taxis for takeoff at
Little Rock AFB, AR. In
addition to three opera-
tional squadrons, the wing
also owns the C-130
"schoolhouse" and the
Combat Aerial Delivery
School, providing graduate
level instruction in C-130
tactical employment.

Opposite page:
A helping hand and a step up are two necessities when working on an aircraft the size of the C-130. Here the crew chief and assistant crew chief install intake and exhaust plugs on one of their charge's T56 engines at the end of another day of flying.

This page:
As the crew chief reviews the aircraft forms, engine specialists unbutton the cowling prior to troubleshooting an engine write-up.

Hercs everywhere! The ramp at Little Rock boasts the world's biggest collection of C-130s. The aircraft in the foreground above shows the Station Keeping Equipment (SKE) antenna above the cockpit. SKE allows C-130 crews to fly formation, and make air drops, in zero/zero weather conditions.

Above: Instrument specialist works a pitot-static write-up with the help of test equipment\par Right: Without the dedicated work of riggers of the 314th Transportation Squadron, nothing would get delivered. All loads destined for air drop, Low Altitude Parachute Extraction (LAPES) or Container Deliver System (CDS) delivery pass through the hands of the riggers.

This page:
All eyes are out front as the C-130 approaches the drop zone. From left to right (at top) there is: the flight engineer, the navigator, the pilot and co-pilot. Meanwhile, (above), the loadmaster monitors the back-end as the extraction chute initiates the vertical portion of the cargo's trip to the drop zone.

Following page:
50th Airlift Squadron C-130H enroute to the drop zone. Typical training sorties usually have low level legs enroute to the drop zone, where SKE formation flying or vis route tactics are practiced. Vis route tactics involve flying as low as 300 feet while utilizing terrain masking to avoid detection.

This page:
While air drops and CDS deliveries can be done in formation, LAPES deliveries are a single ship operation. Here, a C130H delivers a pallet of equipment, literally yanked out the back of the aircraft by parachute, as the C-130 skims the drop zone at about 10 feet and 130 knots. LAPES can deliver up to 42,000 lbs of equipment or supplies.

Following page:
Flying 40,000 hours a year, the 314th keeps the skies around Little Rock full of C-130s most of the time. It takes more than just "shooters" to win a war and the C-130s and their intra-theatre delivery mission perform a vital support function for both the Air Force and Army.

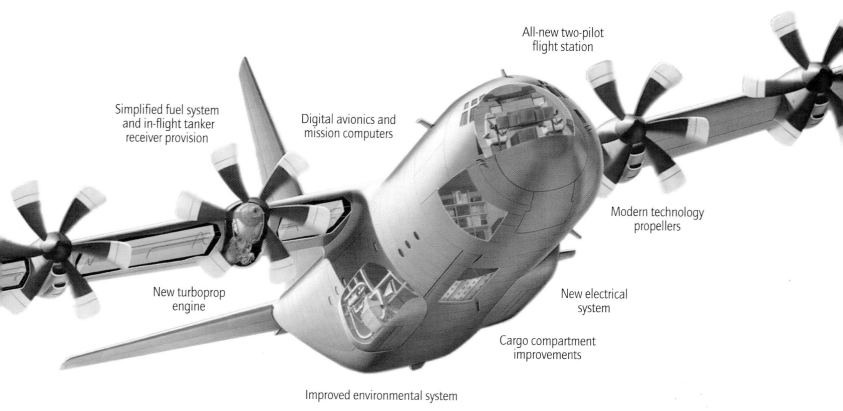

Simplified fuel system
and in-flight tanker
receiver provision

Digital avionics and
mission computers

All-new two-pilot
flight station

Modern technology
propellers

New turboprop
engine

New electrical
system

Cargo compartment
improvements

Improved environmental system

The new J model of the C-130 Hercules airlifter.

It looks just like a C-130.
Until you open it up.

The C-130 is new on the inside. The J model will set a new tactical air mobility standard for an unpredictable world.

New engines and all-composite six-bladed propellers markedly improve the J model's takeoff distance, climb rate, cruise altitude and range. A modernized flight station features electronic displays, controls and on-board mission computers. These cutting edge technologies also lead to significant cost savings. Reductions in the J model's aircrew and maintenance personnel requirements contribute to its 35% annual savings in operating and support costs.

Air mobility must be as good as its name. Only rapid-reaction airlifters like the new C-130J can deliver the force needed to ward off aggression and save lives.

Lockheed leads.

LOCKHEED MARTIN

B-2A of the 509th Bomb Wing takes off from Whiteman AFB, MO; with the aircraft's range, combat sorties will also takeoff and recover at Whiteman. All aspect stealth, long range and an impressive payload - the B-2 gives the United States unique capabilities to deter and respond to aggression. The B-2 is a vital part of our policy of being able to conduct two major wars simultaneously, with it's ability to rapidly shift from one theatre to another.

Left:

B-2 presents a unique profile. Jet is flown by a two man crew. First ten B-2s will be Block 10 jets with limited conventional capabilities, followed by three Block 20 jets with improved capabilities and finally "full-up" Block 30 jets will be delivered starting in 1997. These will include 5 of the 6 flight test aircraft refurbished and upgraded. Earlier Block jets will be upgraded to Block 30 configuration after the last production aircraft is delivered.

Above:

Split ailerons function as "drag rudders" replacing conventional vertical tail surfaces in damping yaw. Deletion of high radar cross section vertical tail surfaces was one of the great accomplishments of the B-2 design team. Another notable achievement, (required to meet stealth capability), was dimensional control during the manufacturing process. Northrop-Grumman developed a manufacturing process that is so rigid that no two B-2s will differ in wingspan by more than a half inch - or two one hundredths of one percent!

This page:
Although it may not seem so, the B-2 is a big aircraft. At 172 feet the wing span is only 13 feet shorter than a B-52's, however its length is 100 feet less - but it's still a big piece of metal. All that metal (and plastic), can carry a large payload. The aircraft can carry more than 140,000 lbs of fuel and 40,000 lbs of ordinance. Side by side weapons bays can be loaded with up to 80

MK-82 500 lb iron bombs, or 16 MK-84/GBU-29 JDAM 2000 lb bombs or 34 CBU-87/89/97s cluster bombs.

Next page:
White spot on the center-line of the aircraft is retractable radar reflector, enabling the B-2 to be seen by peacetime air traffic control radars. Antennas for the APQ-181 "radar(s)" are behind large rectangu-lar panels underneath the

aircraft, just aft of the lead-ing edge and just outboard of the centerline.
"Radar(s)" is the appropri-ate designation since B-2 carries two of the systems - one per side - but the elec-tronics from either side can run both, the cross-con-nected systems are com-pletely redundant. In addi-tion to being stealthy, radar has both full air-to-air and air-to-ground capabilities - it can search for enemy

fighters like an F-16 radar, while "shooting" a SAR map of a suspected target like a B-1 radar.

Following spread: B-2A takes on fuel from a KC-135R of the 155th ARG, Nebraska ANG. Rearward location of the refueling receptacle forces the B-2 to fly well forward on the tanker and, as a result, causes the B-2's bow wave to "push" the KC-135. This makes get-ting "plugged" challenging for both pilots and the boomer. It also explains why the B-2 seen here is at the lower limit of the boom's envelope. Normally, pilots shoot to have the "apple" - the yellow circle in the center of the green section, just visible outside the upper half of the boom.

Page 78: B-2A turns toward Whiteman at the comple-tion of a training mission. B-2s train for both nuclear and conventional opera-tions. Efforts are under-way to equip the "Spirit" with precision guided weapons to improve it's capabilities in the conven-tional arena. Advent of GPS guided GBU-29 Joint Direct Attack Munition (JDAM) will allow the B-2 to make accurate attacks against targets in any weather.

Catch the Spirit

REACH · RESPONSIVENESS · PRECISION · SURVIVABILITY

B-2 SPIRIT

POWER PROJECTION FOR THE 21ST CENTURY

UNITED STATES AIR FORCE · NORTHROP GRUMMAN · B-2 TEAM

NORTHROP GRUMMAN

Previous Page
Eagle over the tidewater. An F-15C of the 1st Wing turns on to initial at Langley AFB, VA. This Eagle is carrying a load similar to that used in DESERT STORM: four AIM-7M radar guided missiles and four AIM-9M heat-seeking missiles. The "First Wing" has three squadrons of F-15Cs assigned at Langley and two rescue squadrons assigned at Patrick AFB, FL. The rescue units are the 41st, flying HH-60Gs and the 71st, flying the HC-130P. Between them, they are flying some of the newest and oldest aircraft in the inventory - the HH-60s being delivered last year and the HC-130s being delivered in 1965.

Lower Right
Post-mission paperwork; pilot and crew chief of the 94th FS fill out the forms. Notice that the patch is missing from the pilot's right shoulder - since you would normally remove velcro mounted patches, "sanitizing" your uniform, prior to a combat mission, many crews do the same in peacetime - you fight like you train.

Upper Left:
With the background, this could have been shot over Nevada or Iraq; the 1st FW, like all ACC units, spends a lot of time on the road. With deployments to training exercises, such as Red Flag (seen here) and "real world" contingency deployments, the average ACC aircrew member, maintainer and support troop spends over 100 days a year away from home.

Four-ship of F-15Cs refuel from Seymour Johnson based KC-10. On a typical combat sortie, an Eagle four-ship might "hit the tanker" repeatedly. Eagles can be tasked with defensive counter air, where they set up CAPs (orbits) over friendly territory to defend that territory or something in/over it (such as tankers or AWACS) or offensive counter air. OCA missions call for the F-15s to sweep in front of, or escort, friendly aircraft into hostile territory. Photo at right shows an Eagle in the pre-contact position, where the pilot stabilizes for a moment prior to moving into the contact position where the boomer "plugs" the jet.

Following Spread: 1st Fighter Wing F-15C shows off its load of four AIM-7s and four AIM-9s. Not seen are the 940 rounds of high explosive incendiary ammunition for the Eagle's 20mm cannon that are carried internally. With the advent of predictor gunsights and longer range PGU-28 ammunition, the 20mm cannon has become an even more lethal component of the F-15's arsenal.

"Number three's turning." As the crew chief monitors the start, an HC-130P of the 71st Rescue Squadron cranks engines prior to flying a training sortie. Using the "King" callsign, these aircraft act as overall mission commanders, coordinating combat search and rescue efforts. Special modifications for this role include pods under the outboard wing section (not seen here) containing hose reel units to refuel helicopters, "picture windows" on the fuselage sides for observers, a beacon tracking antenna and its large radome on the top of the fuselage and a modified nose to accommodate Fulton Recovery System gear. While liquid oxygen boils off, specialist, (left), wears protective clothing while working with "LOX cart." Cart is used to service oxygen system on the aircraft.

the Air Force in not requiring maintenance pre-flight, thru-flight or post flight inspections. Instead, a more rigorous weekly inspection is conducted, as seen here. The aircraft's Army heritage can be seen in the ability to conduct maintenance without special stands - the cowling opens up to form a servicing platform and hand and footholds extend from tail. Modifications for rescue work include a personnel hoist above the main cabin door, a refueling probe on an extendable boom attached to right forward fuselage and a APN-239 weather and ground mapping radar mounted on the left side of the nose.

Like the 71st, the 41st Rescue Squadron's wartime mission, combat search and rescue, mirrors its peacetime mission, which is also providing search and rescue - the only difference being that people normally aren't shooting at them! The 41st is tasked with providing SAR support for all Space Shuttle launches, in addition to supporting deployment and contingency taskings. HH-60 is unique in

Previous page:
Two F-15Es of the 4th Wing at Seymour Johnson AFB, NC, on the way to Dare County Range on the North Carolina coast. Their load consists of 12 MK-82 inerts. With its unequaled combination of range, air-to-air and air-to-ground capabilities, the F-15E is quickly becoming ACC's premier interdiction machine.

Left and right:
Strike Eagles prefer to attack - and so end up training - at night. Night attacks play to the F-15E's strong suit, its combination of sensors that give it unparalleled night precision bombing capability, while greatly complicating the enemies' defensive situation. The sensor suite is comprised of the APG-70 multi-mode radar and the LANTIRN system. LANTIRN is a two pod system, mounted on the belly of the aircraft, that combines a terrain following radar and wide field of view FLIR with a high resolution, steerable IR camera and boresighted laser ranger/designator. Together, these sensors allow the F-15E to operate in the dark just as they would in daytime.

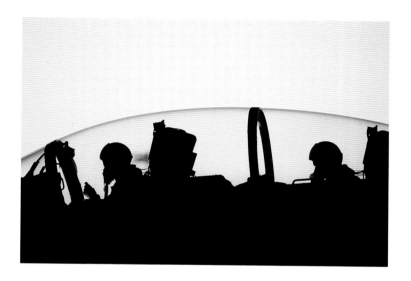

Previous page:

Like all ACC units, 4th Wing F-15Es practice dropping heavyweight ordinance, as well as sub-scale practice munitions. A Strike Eagle crew has a pretty full plate when it comes to training - in addition to range work with unguided weapons there is practice with laser guided bombs and Mavericks, intercept training as well as air-to-air skills to keep honed. (and aerial refueling and low level flying and instrument approaches and....)

Left page:

Following a low level approach to the target, an F-15E "pops" to gain altitude for his dive bomb delivery, which he's rolling in for, here. Dive bombing increases bombing accuracy while complicating AAA gunners tracking solutions. These high threat tactics are demanding and so are practiced frequently.

This page:

F-15E captured in the middle of rippling twelve MK-82 500 lb bombs. One bomb can be seen just leaving the rack. For medium to low threat situations, level attacks from medium altitude are practiced. Attacks such as these are usually cued from the APG-70 radar. After the target area is identified in the ground mapping real beam mode, a synthetic aperture "patch" map of the target area is taken and frozen. The WSO can then study the high resolution image - more like a photograph than a traditional radar picture - to pick out the target or offset aim point, (OAP). Either the target, or a radar significant feature a known distance from the target, (the OAP), is designated and from this the aircraft's computers provide steering and weapons release computations to the crew.

Previous page:
Even with the prodigious range of the F-15E, aerial refueling must be practiced; a five ship of Strike Eagles takes on gas from a KC-10. During DESERT STORM, 4th Wing F-15Es normally flew with their conformal tanks (containing 4,000 lbs of JP-4) and two external 600 gal tanks (8400 more pounds) and still had to refuel.

Left:
Four ship of 335th Fighter Squadron F-15Es enroute to the range. The 4th Wing gave the Strike Eagle its baptism of fire during DESERT STORM - only months after the becoming operational on the new jet. The outstanding contributions the wing made to the war effort are all the more remarkable for the fact that they were still transitioning to their new aircraft.

Above:
"Tangential" weapons stations on the conformal fuel tanks reduce drag when carrying a full load of weapons like the 12 MK-82s seen here. LANTIRN pods are under intakes; targeting pod on the left side and navigation pod on the right. Rails on wing stations can hold either AIM-9, (seen here), or AIM-120 AMRAAMs - or a combination of both.

Following page:
Air-to-air capabilities of earlier F-15 models are retained in the F-15E. The two person Strike Eagle crew has a tremendous capability to fight their way to and from the target area using the track-while-scan APG-70 and AIM-7, AIM-9 and AIM-120 missiles. When enforcing the No-Fly Zones over Bosnia and Iraq, typical loadout for the "Beagle," as aircrews refer to it, is "two by": two AIM-120s, two AIM-7s, two AIM-9s and two laser guided bombs.

F-15E

Air Supremacy

MCDONNELL DOUGLAS

Previous page:
Part of the new thinking that the creation of ACC has brought with it, is the formation of Combined Wings. These wings take a large view of an old TAC adage, you fight the way you train. These units train together and will fight together in wartime. At Shaw Air Force Base, SC, A-10 and F-16s are molded into a team that has Forward Air Control, Close Air Support, Interdiction and Air Defense Suppression capabilities.

This page:
On the F-16 side of the house, the 77th Fighter Squadron provides interdiction and close air support with their F-16Cs while the 78th and 79th Fighter Squadrons flying Block 50D F-16s provides air defense suppression using their HARM Targeting System equipped jets. These airplanes both carry typical loads for their missions; the 77th jet (foreground) armed with two MK-84 2000 lb bombs, while the 78th airplane has two AGM-88 HARM anti-radar missiles. Both jets carry AIM-9M Sidewinders on their wingtips and ALQ-184 ECM pods on their centerline stations.

This page:
No matter how cosmic the jet, it still won't turn a wheel without the dedicated work of alot of people. Above, specialists hustle to fix an hydraulic problem. The FOD can is nearby to receive any stray nuts or wires that would have ended up on the ground - and potentially in the intake of a running jet engine. (Right) Crew chief re-installs a panel after maintenance is completed.

White rubber booties protect the aircraft from being scuffed by boots.

Far right:
Improved wind model in Block 50 F-16 weapons release computer and GPS aided navigation has dramatically improved the "Viper's" accuracy when dropping unguided bombs, such as these MK-84 2000 lb "slicks," from medium altitude.

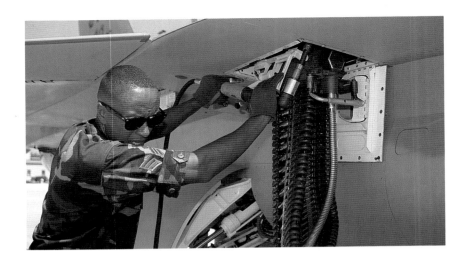

Top left:
Fully accessorized Vipers: AGM-88 HARM mounted on a LAU-88 modified with Launcher Avionics Package (LAP). The LAP allows the F-16 to "talk" to the HARM, passing targeting information to the missile before launch.

Lower photo: AIM-120 and AIM-9M air-to-air missiles grace the 20th Operations Group "Flagship". The all-aspect "heater" (AIM-9) and the fire-and-forget AMRAAM (AIM-120) have made the Viper even more lethal in the air-to-air business. Yellow bands indicate live warheads, while brown bands signify live rocket motors.

Top right:
Munitions troop loads 20mm. Loader has two chutes; as fresh rounds are loaded, spent casings are removed from aircraft. Spent casings are retained in the aircraft for weight and balance purposes as well as to eliminate damage to the jet from dumping brass overboard at 450+ knots.

Facing page:
F-16 pilot of the 77th FS, making a maintenance write-up after a sortie. "Horsecollar" life preserver he wears contains SEWARS system that automatically deploys the preserver when it gets immersed in water. Combined with SEWARS releases for the parachute, this system significantly improves the survival chances of an unconscious pilot in an over water bailout.

This page:
20th Fighter Wing F-16C pilot expends an IR counter-measure flare in a test of the ALE-47 dispenser system. The system carries a mixture of chaff, to decoy radar missiles, and flares, to decoy infrared guided weapons. Pilot can set system to dispense either singles, multiples or groups (for example, three bundles of chaff, a pause, and then three more bundles of chaff). Block 50 F-16 has a "slap" switch mounted on the left cockpit sidewall, above the throttle, as well as a new switch on the stick, to actuate the system.

Right page:
A SAM operator's second worse nightmare, HARM Targeting System (HTS) equipped F-16s on a training sortie near Shaw AFB. While not a full blown Weasel, the HTS provides a significant upgrade to the F-16's air defense suppression capability. Previous F-16/HARM set-ups basically only provided for carriage and launch of the AGM-88 from the Viper. Targeting information

came from a near-by F-4G and reduced the effectiveness of the HARM. Current system provides on-board targeting as well as improved situational awareness displays for the pilot. (Right) HTS sensor occupies the right forward intake station otherwise used by the LANTIRN targeting pod in Block 42/52 Vipers.

Left:
On the A-10 side of the 20th Wing, the Warthogs of the 55th Fighter Squadron provide both Forward Air Control and Close Air Support. Here, a Shaw A-10 strafes at nearby Poinsett range; the GAU-8 cannon putting out 6 feet of smoke in front of the jet along with 30mm shells.

Above:
AGM-65 Maverick being loaded on a 55th FS A-10. To load the missile, munitions personnel remove the LAU-114 launcher from aircraft, open the Maverick's storage container (referred to as a "coffin") and attach the launcher to the missile. The munitions loader then picks up the coffin and hooks the launcher to the aircraft's pylon. This process has just been completed in the photo, with the loader dropping the coffin away from the missile. The rails at the top of the picture are for AIM-9 air-to-air missiles. While not famous as an air-to-air machine, the all-aspect AIM-9s and the "Hogs" nose pointing ability give it a viable self defense capability.

By combining units with complementary assets, composite wings improve peacetime training and wartime combat capability. Units that train together, daily, get to better understand the strengths and weaknesses of each other and learn the unique requirements that the other has. Above an AGM-65 armed A-10 and an AGM-88 armed F-16 return to Shaw AFB after working together in the Gamecock Military Operating Area. The A-10 shown above is serial number 81-964, which on 15 February 1991 shot down an Iraqi MI-8 Hip helicopter with its 30mm gun; accounting for the green star on the aircraft's nose.

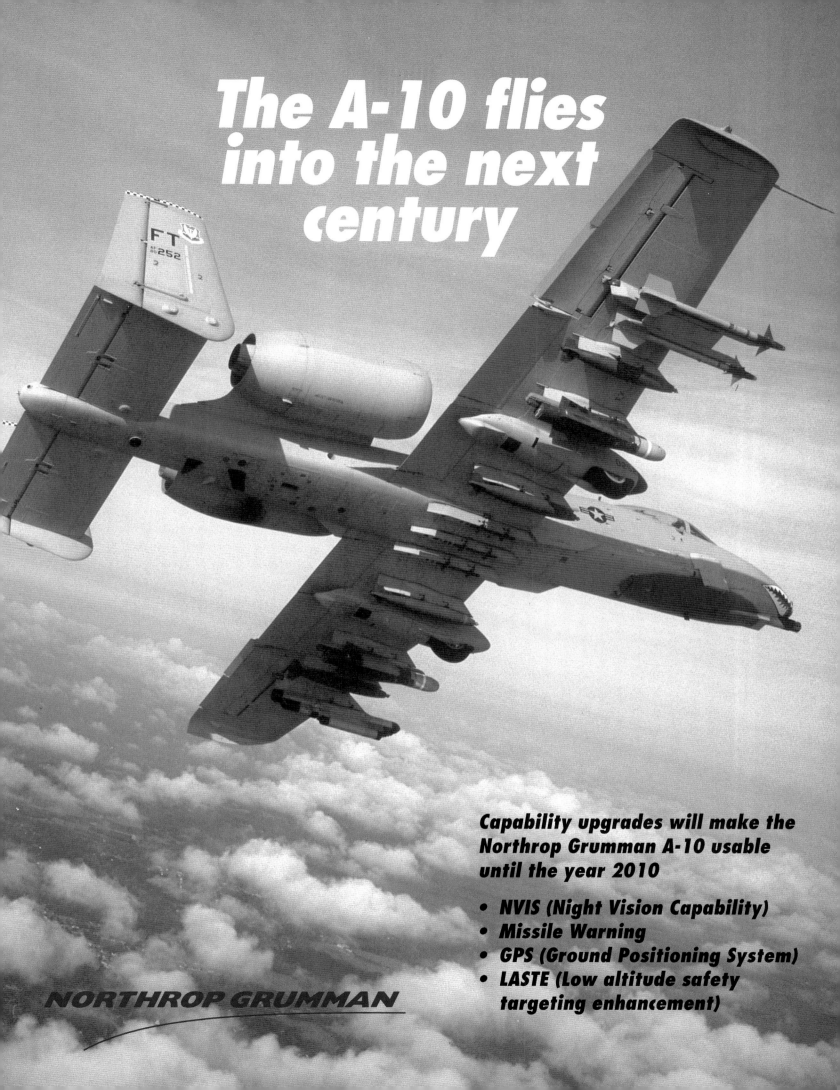

The A-10 flies into the next century

Capability upgrades will make the Northrop Grumman A-10 usable until the year 2010

- **NVIS (Night Vision Capability)**
- **Missile Warning**
- **GPS (Ground Positioning System)**
- **LASTE (Low altitude safety targeting enhancement)**

NORTHROP GRUMMAN

Previous page:
Now that's nose art! C-130H of the 23rd Wing Flying Tigers sports new markings as a part of the Air Force's first Battlefield Support Composite Wing. The 23rd includes C-130s, A-10s and F-16s and is designed to provide firepower and intra-theatre logistical support to ground units - in particular the co-located 82nd Airborne Division.

Left page:
The 23rd's C-130s provide the normal gamut of airlift support - supplying ground units through airland and air drop operations - additionally they see an inordinate amount of "paratrooping" - supplying one way lifts for the airborne troops of Ft Bragg.

This page:
C-130H practicing airland operations at an assault strip on Ft Bragg. Soft, short field operations require a deft touch from the pilots, which calls for frequent practice of these techniques.

Left page:
Everything the 82nd Airborne owns has to be capable of aerial delivery, including heavy equipment - an example of which is seen leaving a Flying Tiger C-130H. The chute that is open is only the extraction chute, to get the cargo out of the "Herc;" the main chutes will deploy momentarily.

This page:
23rd Wing A-10s provide forward air control as well as close air support. This is an OA-10 FAC aircraft, which differs only in designation and mission from a "regular" A-10. Aircraft carries a LAU-68 rocket launcher, holding 2.75" rockets with "willie pete" warheads. The white phosphorus warhead produces a large white cloud on impact and is used to mark targets for attack aircraft. This Warthog also carries an ALQ-184 ECM pod and a Pave Penny pod. Mounted on the short pylon below the cockpit, the Pave Penny pod detects "spots" from laser designators and displays them in the pilot's Heads Up Display. Friendly ground teams and scout helicopters can "paint" enemy positions with their laser designators to help ensure positive target identification.

Next page:
A-10s displaying the "everything AND the kitchen sink" approach to weapons loads. They each have ALQ-184 ECM pods, four MK-82 500 lb "slicks", two AGM-65D IR Mavericks and two AIM-9Ms, plus the incomparable GAU-8 gun with 1150 rounds. Able to stay on station for long periods and highly accu rate with both bombs and the gun, the A-10 is the Army's first choice for close air support.

A-10 rolling in for a dive delivery on a Ft Bragg impact area. Aircraft shows false canopy painted on the belly to confuse AAA gunners and air-to air adversaries as to the Warthogs true attitude. Stain on the bottom of the left engine cowling is caused by the APU exhaust. The A-10 is completely self-contained for starting - a plus when deployed to austere forward airfields.

F-16 rolling in over Ft Bragg. LANTIRN equipped Block 42 F-16 provides an excellent complement to the A-10 with true nighttime capability and significant air-to-air talents. Vipers can swing from mud moving to air-to-air as required by circumstances.

Previous page:
CAS configured F-16s with triple ejector racks (to carry bombs or cluster munitions) on the left wing and TGM-65 Mavericks on the right wing. An ALQ-184 ECM pod is on the centerline and 600 gallons external tanks are on the inboard wing stations. Dark grey LANTIRN pods are mounted below the intakes. Although these pods are clones of those mounted on F-15Es, they are mounted in reverse configuration to those on the Strike Eagle, the Viper has its targeting pod on the right and the Nav pod is on the left.

This page:
Load training - munitions personnel practice loading a CBU-89. Weapon being loaded is physically identical to a live round but has no explosives either in the fuse or the sub-munitions. This allows a little more leeway when inexperienced hands deal with a 750 lb "training aid".
Munitions troops must be certified, and constantly trained with, each of the 13 types of ordinance the F-16 can haul into battle. The CBU-89 is one of three weapons based on the tactical munitions dispenser. The TMD provides a standardized container for a variety of sub-munitions which simplifies loading and handling. The TMD is also a big step up from previous CBU "cans" as it has an improved radar proximity fuse (with ECCM features and selectable height of burst) and a tail section that can cant after release to spin the weapon (at variable rates) prior to releasing the sub-munitions; a pretty cosmic "can". Sub-munition for
the -89 is the Gator mine. This is actually two different types of mines - one anti-armor, the other anti-personnel - packed together in the same CBU.

GLOBAL REACH
GLOBAL POWER...

SENSOR FUZED WEAPON
IS ON THE TEAM

TEXTRON Defense Systems

Textron Defense Systems/Subsidiary of Textron Inc.,
201 Lowell Street Wilmington, MA 01887

Previous page:
Four ship of F-15Cs from the 33rd Fighter Wing over their home, Eglin AFB, FL. The 33rd was extremely successful during DESERT STORM, downing 16 Iraqi aircraft, more than any other allied unit. Seen here with the current standard load-out for F-15Cs - two AIM-7s, four AIM-120s and two AIM-9s - during the war these jets flew "four by four" - four AIM-7s and four AIM-9s. If the AIM-120 had been out of development in time to go to the war, the 33rd's kill rate would have been significantly higher due to the expanded envelope of the AMRAAM vs the Sparrow.

Facing page:
A prime ingredient in the 33rd's success was (and is) the efforts of their maintenance personnel, seen here working to fix a stab actuator problem. Rivet Workforce effort has made ACC maintainers more versatile, cross-training them among specialties which gives supervisors more flexibility in assigning them to work aircraft problems.

This page:
Referring to the "T.O.s", a supervisor and an engine troop work to solve a "motor" write-up. Use and adherence to Tech Orders is an important part of ACC's flying safety program. Efforts in recent years have reduced logistics related mishaps - which include maintenance factors - to all time lows.

This page:
Pilot "mounts up" for another training sortie at Eglin. No, that's not a very small parachute on his back. Lumbar pad contains a tree lowering device; 150 feet of nylon rope with a belaying device that connects to the pilot's harness. If the pilot has to bail out and has the double misfortune of the parachute snagging in a tree, then one end of the rope attaches to the parachute, the belay goes on the harness and after releasing him (or her) self from the chute, the pilot slowly gets lowered to the ground.

Above:
58th Fighter Squadron F-15Cs get their "last chance" inspection at EOR. Jet in foreground, serial number 85-0114 is the one that Capt Caesar Rodriguez splashed two Iraqi MiGs: a MiG-29 on January 19th and a MiG-23 on January 26th, 1991. Both kills were achieved with radar guided AIM-7M Sparrows.

Left:
Tradition in action - the crew chief always helps his pilot strap-in the jet and always sends him off with a sharp salute as he taxis out. Dedication of typically young, smart maintainers is amazing. Working long hours in tough conditions, their biggest reward is often only satisfaction in a job well done - but occasionally includes painting kill markings on their jet.

Facing page:
Air-to-air gunnery is a demanding art, recently made easier by the use of radar-aided "predictor" gunsights. To practice this art, fancy gunsights or not, F-15s tow the AGTS-36 target. The target is attached by steel cable to the reel unit which in turn is latched to the Eagle's centerline station. Once in restricted airspace, the pilot

plays out 2000 feet of cable and goes into a constant turn (or climbing and diving turn for "combat" profiles). Other F-15s then come in and take turns honing their gunnery skills. The AGTS-36 target has an acoustical scoring device attached to it that records the number of bullets that pass through an area about the size of an average fighter - no counting holes in the gunnery banner any more! When practice is complete, the tow pilot reels in the target, the reel unit contains a small wind driven turbine for this purpose.

Following page:
Two 33rd FW F-15s fly through their practice areas south of the Florida panhandle. Extensive restricted and warning areas controlled by Eglin and Tyndall provide excellent training opportunities. Airspace for everything from simple intercepts to live fire of air-to-air missiles is available, along with an Air Combat Maneuvering Instrumentation Range. Airspace is heavily utilized and scheduling is sometimes a problem, with users from the test activities of Material Command at Eglin and Air Education and Training Command F-15 training unit students competing with the 33rd and other users for the airspace.

Facing page:
F-16 pilot of the 347th Wing and his mount on the ramp at Moody AFB, GA. 347th is ramping up ACC's second Battlefield Support Composite Wing. Three squadrons of F-16s are soon to give way to two F-16 squadrons, an A-10 squadron and a C-130 squadron. The grey hose seen between the horsecollar is part of the Combat Edge anti-G vest. Combat Edge system incorporates a new fast acting g-suit valve with the anti-g vest and a positive pressure oxygen regulator. The system vastly improves pilot's G tolerance and comfort. This is more important than ever since latest Block 50/52 Vipers can not only pull 9 Gs, they can sustain them...while accelerating.

This page:
Moody's F-16s are LANTIRN equipped, so dusk takeoffs are a common sight at this South Georgia base. While some LANTIRN training can be accomplished during daylight hours, the best quality work is to be found after dark. LANTIRN system ties into the autopilot, allowing low levels to be flown hands-off at 100 feet AGL. These are followed by range work using the APG-68 radar and the LANTIRN targeting pod.

This page:
EOR crews hustle to get "last chance" inspections accomplished and weapon safety pins pulled. This F-16 is headed for the range with 6 BDU-33 practice bombs in the SUU-20 dispenser under his right wing. A slow EOR crew can result in late take-offs which puts training at risk; tanker, low-level and range times are all scheduled and being late might mean not getting valuable training.

This page:
Not all training including aircrews is for aircrews. Here, an F-16 pilot, pretending to be unconscious, is "rescued" by a firefighter during a ground emergency drill. While their brethren douse the simulated fire, firefighters open the Viper's canopy manual ly, (a not-so-fun exercise involving a speed wrench and what seems like an hour of cranking), safe the ejection seat, unhook the pilot from the eight different connections that mate him to the jet and then yank him out. Advent of more petite female fighter pilots was warmly welcomed by firefighters.

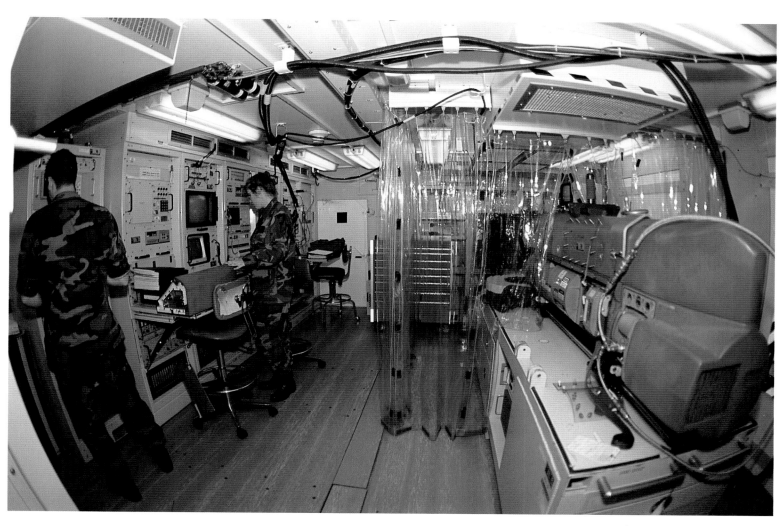

This page:
"Pilots break'em, we fix'em." Modular, deployable LANTIRN pod shop fixs'em. Rush to get LANTIRN pods in the field for DESERT STORM resulted in some pods being unique - with non-interchangeable parts. Although factory rework of pods since the war has virtually eliminated this problem, pod shops put in alot of long hours working difficult-to-trouble-shoot, one-of-a-kind pods.

This page:
While Moody crews have several ranges that they use in Georgia and Florida, the Grand Bay Weapons Range, run by the wing has to be the ultimate in convenience. It's only 5 miles from the end of the runway; a pilot can almost takeoff, retract the gear and call base for his first event. Strafe, however, is normally flown as the last event during range work. With the gun mounted directly beside his left ear, the F-16 pilot has no question when it's firing, and leaving the distinctive smoke trail behind the jet.

...combat readiness,

**Link proudly
serves the men and
women of ACC with
excellence in
training systems.**

HUGHES TRAINING, INC.
Link Division

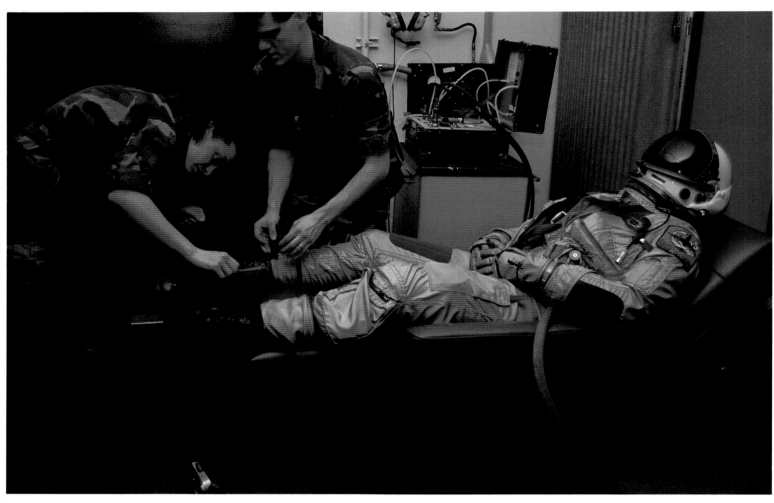

Previous page:
U-2R of the 1st
Reconnaissance Wing
"breaks" for landing over
its home at Beale AFB,
CA. U-2's long range,
long endurance and high
altitude capabilities combined with a versatile sensor suite make it an irreplaceable asset for ACC.
As the only manned (read
flexible) reconnaissance
system left in the Air Force
inventory, the U-2 is highly
tasked to support opera-
tions in every theatre.
Forward operating loca-
tions world-wide put any
point on the globe only a
few hours away from
observation by U-2 sen-
sors. During Desert Storm,
the U-2 was the workhorse
of aerial reconnaissance,
being used both strategical-
ly and tactically. However,
due to the nature of the

"Dragon Lady's" mission, the Air Force did not officially admit system was used in the war until over a year later.

This page and facing page: While pre-breathing pure oxygen, U-2 pilot's pressure suit receives the attention of two Physiological Support Division (PSD) technicians. Pilots must pre-breath to purge nitro- gen from their bloodstream and lessen the possibility of getting the "bends" dur- ing the rapid ascent to operational altitudes. The environment that U-2 pilots frequent, above 70,000 feet, is so demanding that life support functions take on added emphasis. Once all preparations are com- plete, PSD personnel escort the pilot to the jet.

Pressure suit is so bulky and awkward that anything that can be done by some- one else for the pilot - is done; such as carrying the portable cooling unit that ventilates the suit. While the pilot is pre-breathing, the "mobile officer," is preflighting his aircraft, and on the pilot's arrival at the jet, straps him into it. Mobile officer is back-up pilot for today's mission and primary pilot for tomorrow's. Once ensconced in the cockpit, the pilot's work really starts - the U-2 is definitely 1950s technology, cockpit ergonomics are - at best - poor and missions last from 9 to 12 hours.

This page:
U-2R in the instrument pattern during a training sortie. While the jet has a graceful appearance, it's a bear to fly at low altitude. Throw in some cross winds, turbulence and the difficulty of moving around in a pressure suit and it's easy to understand why pilots must have 1500 hours (bomber/transport time or 900 hours fighter/trainer time) before applying to fly the U-2. Most pilots who don't successfully complete the training program wash out because of patterns and landings. Aircraft must be flown to a full stall landing about a foot above the runway - just like any tail wheel aircraft. If the aircraft stalls too high (above 4 feet) structural damage is likely due to light construction of aircraft; if the aircraft is flown on without a stall, the tail wheel won't touch down and directional control is limited. This often is followed by the U-2 departing the runway at an unintended location.

This page:
In an effort to help the pilot during landings, mobile officer in a chase car, (a 5.0 liter Mustang) follows the U-2 down the runway and radios altitude, drift and other information to the pilot. Bicycle landing gear was a compromise the Skunk Works had to make when designing the airplane. Detachable "pogo" outriggers balance the wings for takeoff, but then fall off. After landing, the pilot stops and maintainers re-install them for taxi back. Gaps in wing flaps are for "superpods" - extra sensor bays that can be attached to the wings. They are normally only flown on operational missions. Aircraft seen here is one of the two seat trainers with a position for the instructor pilot added above and behind the regular cockpit.

OUR SIGNATURE AIRCRAFT DOESN'T HAVE ONE.

Building the world's first operational stealth fighter was a challenge for any company. Designed to appear virtually invisible to enemy radar, the F-117A revolutionized the concept of aerial warfare in Desert Storm. The F-117A symbolizes what the Skunk Works® is all about, but it's only one of many breakthrough programs we've executed successfully. Programs like the U-2 high-altitude reconnaissance aircraft, and the triple-sonic SR-71. Which is why when a program like the Stealth Fighter comes along, the Skunk Works comes to mind. When it has to be quick, quiet, and cost-effective, it has our name written all over it. The Skunk Works. An American original since 1943.

LOCKHEED MARTIN

Facing page:

49th Fighter Wing F-117 about to take the runway at Holloman AFB. The F-117 has an importance out of proportion to its small numbers; the aircraft's stealth and precision bombing capabilities make it a primary player in contingency plans world-wide. As one Air Force officer has stated "the Black Jet is really only good for one thing...but its VERY good at that, just ask the Iraqis".

This page:

EOR crews finish their "last chance" inspection before an F-117 departs for the range. For peacetime training the "Black Jet" carries the ubiquitous SUU-20 pod and it's six BDU-33 practice bombs in the weapons bay. While the BDU-33 lacks a laser guidance kit, pilots still get practice in identifying the target, locking on the DLIR (downward looking IR system) and seeing how accurate they, and the jet, are. Aircraft's weapons release computer takes information from the central air data computer, (airspeed, altitude, attitude), INS, (position, drift and acceleration) and DLIR (Angle and range to target), and using stored ballistics tables calculates the bomb release point.

Following page:

Turning initial for Runway 07 at Holloman, F-117 flies over White Sands National Monument. 49th FW markings on the tail mark this as the wing "Flagship", the "personal" aircraft of the wing commander. In actuality aircraft is flown by many pilots, the wing commander being one of them. Typically he would be guaranteed of flying this aircraft on deployments, or when he has to go on temporary duty (TDY), otherwise he is just as likely to fly other aircraft.

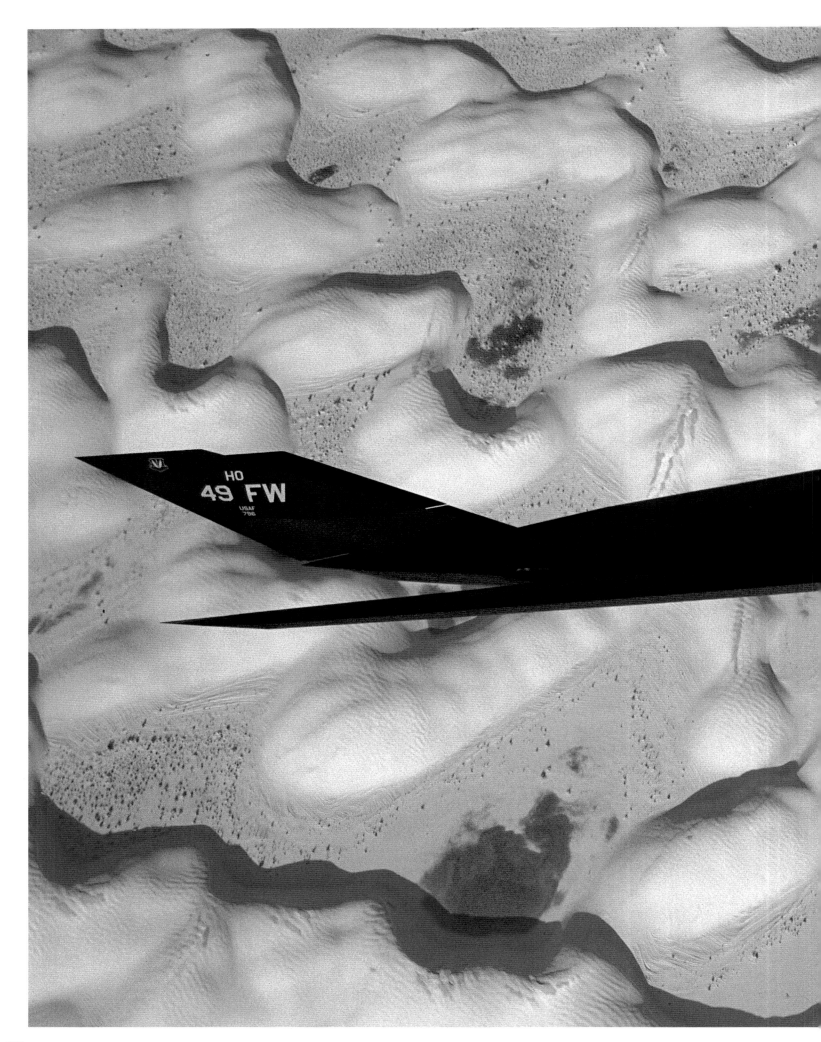

CAPT DAN DECAMP

159

Previous page:
Departing Holloman, a F-117 heads north for bombing practice at Oscura range. Weapons bay doors can be seen in the center of the fuselage with recess for DLIR forward of that. Red markings remind maintenance personnel to avoid the area where the arresting hook would come out if deployed. Rotating beacon under forward fuselage is a bolt-on peacetime item that would be removed prior to combat.

This page:
AT-38 companion trainer chases F-117 student pilot during pattern work. With no two-place F-117s, pilot's first sortie is also his first solo; instructors fly chase to monitor/critique as required. AT-38s once provided fighter lead-in training at Holloman, taking newly graduated pilots and giving them their first taste of bombing and air-to-air training. This training is now conducted at pilot training bases, the AT-38s being disbursed to AETC.

This page:

F-4E of the 20th Fighter Squadron. The last F-4s in the U.S. military, these aircraft provide transition training to German F-4 pilots. Under contract to the Luftwaffe, this training should see the F-4 flying under ACC auspices past the year 2000. In addition to providing transition training, the 20th also runs a graduate school, holding two weapons school classes every year that graduate fighter weapons instructors for the Luftwaffe.

Previous page:

The RC-135s of the 55th Wing are one of the best illustrations of what ACC is all about. Developed to ferret out, (pun intended), the electronic secrets of the Soviet Union, the 55th Wing has become a national asset that is ready to contribute to warfare at any level. Above, an RC-135V of the 55th Wing on a training flight near its home, Offutt AFB, NE. Huge U.S. Air Force caption on the fuselage side is a remnant of the days the RCs spent trolling just outside the borders of the Soviet Union. The Wing's heavily modified "Rivet Joint" aircraft have had tons of equipment added, allowing them to intercept, analyze, record and determine the origin of electronic signals across a broad spectrum. The antennas that gather all these emissions give the RCs a unique look with extended noses, huge "cheek" antenna arrays on the fuselage sides and a veritable "antenna farm" on the aircraft's belly. Married to all the high tech gear are linguists and analysts who are an integral part of the RC's mission crew. Working in the "back end", (as opposed to the "front end," cockpit, crew), these experts provide near-real-time exploitation of signals, providing vital intelligence to users that range from fighter units to the National Command Authorities.

This page:

RC-135V shows some of the antennas added to its former tanker airframe, enabling it to conduct the electronic intelligence gathering mission. RC-135s were heavily tasked during DESERT STORM, providing round the clock coverage of the Kuwaiti theater. Their information was used both by the staff in Riyadh and by airborne aircraft. "Traffic" RC-135s intercepted allowed fighter aircrews to fly safer, more effective missions. Rivet Joint data was used in developing each days Air Tasking Order and in execution of missions ranging from Scud hunting to close air support. An example of the "RJ's" effectiveness was seen on December 27, 1992, when an RC-135 and its 25 man crew, flying in support of SOUTHERN WATCH operations in Southern Iraq, detected a MiG-25 Foxbat flying south toward the 32nd parallel. They passed this information to AWACS, allowing it to track the Foxbat, which it had not previously detected. AWACS Weapons Controllers, in turn, vectored two F-16s on the aircraft when it violated the "no-fly" zone; the resulting kill was directly due to the RJ crew's reporting

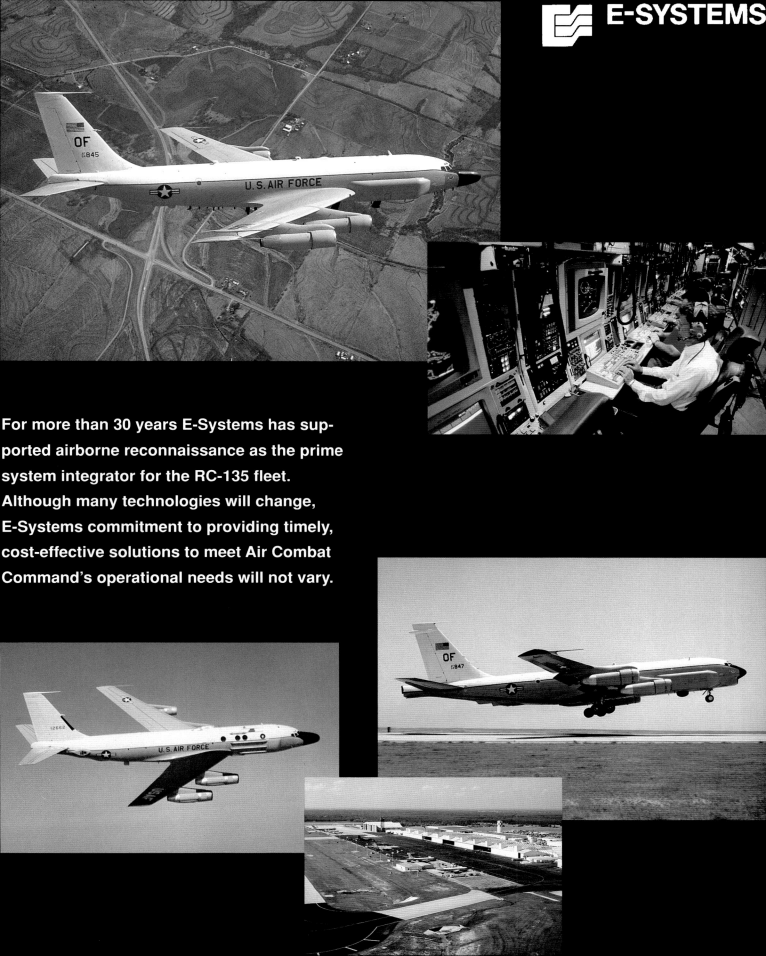

E-SYSTEMS

For more than 30 years E-Systems has supported airborne reconnaissance as the prime system integrator for the RC-135 fleet. Although many technologies will change, E-Systems commitment to providing timely, cost-effective solutions to meet Air Combat Command's operational needs will not vary.

This page:

In addition to composite wings - wings made up of different aircraft that train, deploy and go to war together - there are also combined wings in ACC. Combined wings have different types of aircraft assigned, but do not expect to deploy and fight as a unit. Such is the case at Davis Monthan AFB, AZ. "D-M" is the home of the 355th Wing, composed of the 354th, 357th and 358th Fighter Squadrons flying the A-10, the 41st and 43rd Electronic Combat Squadrons flying the EC-130H and the 42nd Airborne Command and Control Squadron flying the EC-130E. Of the A-10 units, the 354th FS has an operational mission, while the 357th and 358th run the A-10 "schoolhouse," training pilots in the ways of the Warthog. The A-10 is as big as it is ugly. 357th student pilot mounting up, (above), and taxing to EOR, (left), shows just how big the Warthog is.

This page:
In fighters, the basic warfighting unit is the element - 2 airplanes that fly and fight as one. This provides increased firepower and mutual support, and, in turn, drives the training that is conducted. Everything that one airplane can do, two have to be able to do, together. Formation take-offs and landings are practiced to allow the maximum number of airplanes to get airborne or recover in the minimum amount of time (and besides, they're fun). Here, two 358th FS A-10s launch from D-M, while, waiting his turn to take-off, an instructor pilot of the 357th completes his before take-off checklist in EOR.

Facing page:
Maneuvering over the Barry Goldwater range in southwest Arizona, an A-10 pilot of the 357th FS rolls in to drop practice ordinance. Visual bombing is the Warthog's stock in trade - and without a radar, it's the ONLY type of bombing they practice! Recent modifications to the A-10 have made the aircraft, already renowned for its accuracy, an even more deadly bomber. The Low Altitude Safety and Targeting Enhancement system added a Continuous Computed Impact Point presentation to the heads up display, significantly reducing the pilot's workload while dropping ordinance.

This page:
EC-130H (Compass Call) starting engines. Airborne Maintenance Technician (AMT) monitors the start from outside while the crew chief acts as fire guard, manning the fire bottle, "just in case". Comm cord and headset allow the AMT to talk to the flight deck, giving the pilots a better "view" of what's happening. Compass Call aircraft are modified to carry intercept and jamming equipment to disrupt enemy command and control links.

Following page:
EC-130H (Compass Call) of the 41st ECS departs "D-M" on the first leg of an overseas deployment. The Air Force has consolidated all Compass Call aircraft at Davis-Monthan, so the squadrons live on the road supporting contingency operations and training deployments around the globe. Some of the Compass Call modifications to the basic C-130H airframe can be seen here: Antenna array on the aircraft's tail; antenna fairings on the fuselage sides and landing gear fairings extended forward to house additional cooling units with heat exchangers under wings. What can't be seen are all the additional electronic equipment these antennas and cooling units are attached. Almost entirely filling the cargo compartment of the EC-130H, they give the Compass Call an unequaled ability to jam communications links.

This page:
Maintainers minister to one of their charges on the Compass Call ramp at D-M. EC-130Hs perform their mission at medium altitudes, orbiting on the friendly side of the FEBA, which drove aircraft to light grey camouflage scheme seen in the background. Difficulty in maintaining this paint scheme along with the fact that it highlighted the aircraft as a high-value target to the enemy, has forced ACC to repaint the Compass Call fleet in darker colors seen in the foreground.

Facing page:
EC-130H returns to D-M at the completion of a training mission. While training for the "front end" flight crew is fairly straight forward, training for the "back end" mission crew is quite complex - and made difficult by the need to conceal the aircraft's true capabilities during peacetime. Using but a fraction of their full wartime "bag of tricks," **Compass Call** crews still participate with other ACC aircrews in exercises such as Red and Green Flag and other large scale exercises.

This page:

EC-130E of the 42nd ACCS takes off to practice its Airborne Battlefield Command and Control (ABCCC) mission. Aircraft carries a 40 foot long "capsule" that fills the cargo bay of the aircraft. Capsule has 23 radios allowing its mission crew of 12 to control tactical operations of fighters while coordinating air operations with Army and Air Force headquarters elements. On the aircraft above you can see the prominent HF probe antennas under each wing as well as the heat exchanger on the fuselage side, added to cool the capsule's extensive electronics fit. Capsules have recently been upgraded, replacing paper maps and china marker boards with computer screens. Seen below is the mission crew simulator, an exact duplicate of the sophisticated ABCCC III capsule, which allows mission crew members to train while saving valuable flying time.

THE F-16.
AIR TO EVERYTHING.

LOCKHEED MARTIN

Previous page:
Mountain Home AFB, ID
is the home of the Air
Force's first air interdiction
composite unit - the 366th
Wing. Almost an air force
in itself, the wing owns
F-15Cs and Es, F-16s, B-1s
and KC-135s, and is the
first unit to have all the
assets required to conduct
interdiction operations
under one roof. Shown
here are representatives of
each of the wing's five
squadrons: a KC-135R of
the 22nd Air Refueling
Squadron leads, (inboard to
outboard), F-15Cs of the
390th Fighter Squadron,
F-15Es of the 391st Fighter
Squadron and F-16Cs of
the 389 Fighter Squadron
with a B-1B of the 34th
Bomb Squadron in the pre-
contact position, just off
the boom.

This page:
Crew chief and assistant
check out a hydraulic leak
on a 390 FS F-15C. ACC
maintainers work two main
shifts during peacetime
with a skeleton graveyard
shift. During wartime,
maintainers work around
the clock, as required, to
"make it happen." Aircraft
carries a McDonnell
Douglas 600 gal external
tank on the centerline station. Unlike previous
external tanks, this one is
cleared to aircraft "G" limits once empty. Older
tanks had to be jettisoned
when empty because 2 - 3
G limit unnecessarily con-
strained maneuvering.
During DESERT STORM
F-15s did occasionally jet-
tison tanks to minimize
drag/maximize airspeed
when chasing enemy
aircraft.

Facing page:
F-15C over the Clearwater
Mountains north of
Mountain Home AFB.
390th FS F-15s are the
only fighters in the Air
Force equipped with
JTIDS, the Joint Tactical
Information Distribution
System. JTIDS is a secure,
jam resistant, data link that
promises to revolutionize
fighter tactics. The system
simultaneously displays
surveillance information,
(the AWACS "air picture")
while sharing position,
identity and status information among all JTIDS net
users. All the information
that had to pass over voice
radio is now available on a
cockpit display. AWACS
weapons controllers used
to have to "paint the pilots
a picture with words," an
art form, not mastered by

all, that was subject to considerable confusion. Now,
the F-15 pilot has the very
same display as the
weapons controller, with-
out all the verbal and men-
tal gymnastics. Instead of
sorting out who said what
on multiple radios (all
invariably transmitting
simultaneously) and having
to query wingmen on
where they are, what
they're doing and what
their gas and weapon status
is (one wingman at a time)
all the flightlead has to do
now is glance at his dis-
play. The increase in situation awareness is incredible
and promises to provide a
significant improvement in
the F-15's effectiveness.

The mission of 390 FS F-15Cs, such as these, are to provide air superiority where and when required. Typical missions will have some Eagles protecting friendly territory and assets against incursion by enemy fighters, while others will accompany strikers to their targets. Eagles will sweep the striker's route and target area to remove any enemy aircraft and then can go into barrier CAPs (BARCAP) - orbits between the friendlies and anticipated enemy locations. BARCAPs are designed to prevent enemy fighters from disrupting attacks during their most vulnerable time - from IP to bombs away.

Facing page:
Dispensing flares while going vertical, an F-15C pilot tests his ALE-45 chaff and flare system. Self-defense expendables have been a long sought-after item in the F-15 community and have been an add-on modification completed only recently. Part of the challenge of adding this system to the F-15 was the need to develop a larger flare capable of masking the tremendous heat source of the Eagle's two F-100 engines.

McDonnell Douglas F-15Es provide long range precision interdiction platforms to the 366th Wing. While the Strike Eagle's forte is night delivery of precision guided weapons using its LANTIRN system, the "Mud Hen" can also tote major quantities of "pig iron" and deliver it visually during daylight hours. This capability is well illustrated by the jets at the right which are seen with four MK-84 2000 lb bombs, along with four AIM-9Ms for self protection. The MK-84s are on their way to a new owner, below, being rippled off above Owyhee Range in Southwest Idaho. F-15E crew, above, in front of their mount with a load made for tank plinking - eight GBU-12 500 lb laser guided bombs with two AIM-120 AMRAAMs and two AIM-9Ms for self protection. Tank plinking was a concept developed during the Gulf War where individual tanks are destroyed with laser guided bombs; a time consuming process, but very effective.

Previous page:

More robust targets call for more robust bombs. The 391st F-15Es are each hauling four GBU-10 2000 lb laser guided bombs and four AIM-9Ms. The GBU-10 is good against hardened aircraft shelters, bunkers and bridges. For even tougher targets there is the GBU-24 with the BLU-109 warhead, which can punch through six feet of concrete before exploding. Although 8000 lbs of bombs (and 800 lbs of missiles) is a pretty good load, Strike Eagle can haul up to 7 MK-84s (or 14,000 lbs of bombs) but does so at the expense of reduced range.

Facing page and this page:

Air Interdiction Wing in action. As the last F-16 tops off his tanks, the package gets ready to "push" into enemy territory. F-15Cs (light grey) will sweep ahead of the package while F-16s suppress enemy air defenses to get F-15E bombers to their targets. 389th FS flying Block 50D F-16s have the HARM targeting system with which to employ their AGM-88s. F-16 above also carries an ALQ-131 pod and two AIM-9Ms. Despite advent of stealth technology, air defense suppression is as vital as ever. Due to cost, only a small percentage of the Air Force line-up can be stealthy, and non-stealth players must have some form of Weasel. This is especially true with the proliferation of sophisticated air defense systems available on the world market since the collapse of the Soviet Union.

Previous page:

Advantage of true multi-role aircraft, such as these Lockheed-Martin F-16s, is their ability to be used against whichever "fire is hotter." Commanders have the ability to use the airplanes as Weasels, Air-to-Air players, Close Air Support assets, or Interdiction machines, depending on where the need is greatest - and expect them to perform well in any of those roles. These 389th FS jets carry AGM-65B Mavericks, which are useful in all the roles listed above, except for Air-to-Air. "B" model uses TV guidance, "D" model swaps TV seeker for an imaging infrared seeker which gives greater daytime launch ranges and allows nighttime operations. New "G" model Maverick provides the same day/night capability as the "D" model with a warhead almost twice the size of the older weapon.

This page:

The irreplaceable support asset is the tanker. No matter how long your legs are it seems like you always need more gas. Here are two different perspectives on the same operation. For the fighters half the fun is just getting there. Comm out tanker rendezvous may seem like an easy operation in an aircraft equipped with radar and capable of maneuvering much better and flying much faster, but appearances can be deceiving. Tankers don't always fly neat orbits, sometimes opting for more tactical random patterns in the airspace they're allotted. And you can't rejoin on just any tanker - only the one you've been assigned to. Tanker offloads take a great deal of planning to make sure everyone in the package gets the gas they need from what's available, in the time allotted. Going to the wrong tanker can completely screw up a mission. Throw in some weather and an unanticipated turn by the tankers and you may be on the receiving end of a "high aspect" tanker rejoin, (otherwise known as being 180 out with the tanker at the rejoin). Then, after you get to the boom, you've got to get plugged, which can take place in a turn while squinting into the sun. When

you've got sunlight conditions such as these, or when the sun is reflected off an undercast, the director lights can't be seen which dramatically increases the pilots (and boomers) workload. With no director lights, the pilot has to guess where to put the jet and hope that the boomer will "stick" him ..... quickly. Even with the director lights, "hanging on the boom" can be a challenge in weather or turbulence. Un-refueled wingmen go to the right wing and cycle through to the left wing after getting gas.

This page:

Since no tankers equals no mission for anybody, half the tanker's job is simply to be there, where and when called for. The KC-135's navigator's job is to ensure on time arrival at the track, then to keep the cell (group of tankers) within the confines of the track. Working with the pilots, he or she must try to keep everyone out of the worst of the weather, but in the assigned airspace, (which accounts for some of those unexpected turns the fighters curse about) and must have the tanker back at the air refueling initial point at the control time for each group of receivers the tanker has. Since a stable platform is as important for the boomer as it is the fighters, most of the time in the tanker track is spent on autopilot. With autopilot failures reasonably common, pilots get plenty of practice concentrating on instruments for long periods of time. As the fighters join up, the boomer comes into play. Lying on his stomach in the ventral pod, almost at the aft end of the fuselage, the boomer flies the boom into the fighter's receptacle with a control stick located just to the right and below the platform he's lying on. The boom does not response quickly to control inputs and plugging a receiver can be tough - especially when the receiver can't see the director lights or when there's turbulence or simply when the receiver is a new pilot. Co-pilot monitors the amount of off-load and advises the boomer when to disconnect, so everyone receives the proper amount of fuel. Team work is essential to a successful tanker mission.

This page:
More than any other unit, Mountain Home practices integrating bombers into interdiction packages. The 34th Bomb Squadron's B-1s are based off station, at Ellsworth AFB, SD, but with the "Bone's" legs, this isn't a problem. With its maneuverability and speed, the B-1 is fairly easy to integrate into strike packages, while its payload makes it a valued member of the team. Presently, the B-1 is limited to MK-82 "iron" bombs, but could carry GBU-12s, if another aircraft designated the target. B-1 bomb racks are being modified to carry Tactical Munitions Dispensers, (TMDs), which means the jet will soon be able to deliver 30 1000 lb CBU-87/89/97s, all of which are based on the TMD. The GPS guided GBU-29 Joint Direct Attack Munition is also on tap, but won't be fielded on the B-1 until 2001.

Following page:
366th Wing will be one of the first units deployed the next time a DESERT STORM - like scenario develops. But this time units won't need months to spin up and master working together - they will have been doing it for years.

PRECISION STRIKE

"When survivability depends on accuracy"

ADVANCED BORESIGHT EQUIPMENT

machine. While most weapons are loaded with the "assistance" of the MJ-1B "jammer," 200 lb AIM-9s are loaded by the method you see here - three each munitions troops and sweat.

This page, below: MK-82s show their M904 fuses mounted in the nose of the weapon. Arming wires can be seen attached to the vane on the front of the fuse. These wires are tied off to the aircraft and prevent the vanes from spinning until the bomb comes off the aircraft. The fuses arm after the vanes spin a preset number of times. Routing and security of the arming wires are a high interest item during preflight, and a "spinner" check is done by the pilot after takeoff to visually confirm that none of the vanes are rotating.

Facing page:
The first thing every pilot does on every sortie is check the forms. The "781" contains the records of aircraft flying time, servicing, inspections finished and required, discrepancy write-ups, and modifications accomplished and remaining. The crew chief is responsible for keeping the forms up to speed and ensuring that everything is "signed off" prior to flight.

This page, above:
In the words of an Air Force officer, "Without ordinance, ACC would be just another unscheduled airline." Without munitions troops to load that ordinance, ACC wouldn't be any closer than that to being a war-winning

Facing page:
About to "drop live", the flightlead gets permission from the range controller to enter restricted airspace. For training, including live ordinance deliveries, Hill units use the Utah Test and Training Range (UTTR), an outstanding facility southwest of Salt Lake City. Since keeping the radios free for critical calls, (such as "Ram 2, Break Left! MiG, 5 O'clock, 6000 feet!), is a priority, pilots use aircraft motions and hand signals to communicate in some instances, much as they did in World War One. Here, the flightlead wanted to get a fuel check prior to entering

the range. He rocked his wings, signalling the wingman to move into route formation, then with a hand signal asked the wingman his fuel status. Wingman responded with a hand signal and the flightlead will shortly "porpoise" his jet telling the wingman to return to tactical formation. (The green apparition between the two jets is actually a reflection of the radar scope on the canopy).

This page:
Bombs Away! 4th FS F-16C ripples six MK-82s over UTTR. Bombs are released from one side and then the other, causing the jet to rock back and forth

during a ripple release. Bombs gone, the pilot comes in with 4 to 5 "Gs" to pull away from the target and the impending explosions in its vicinity. Coming off target, the pilot uses his radar to expedite a rejoin on his flightlead.

This and facing page:
In a scene that could be right out of DESERT STORM, a 388th F-16 unleashes two MK-82s over UTTR. "Airfield" in the background is another UTTR target. During the Gulf War, 388th F-16s performed fast FAC "Killer Scout" missions, identifying and confirming destruction of Iraqi targets.

Aircraft flew with six MK-82s, just as seen here. Orbiting at 15,000 feet, Killer Scouts would use binoculars to search for Iraqi army units. They would then roll in and mark them with a MK-82, calling in additional fighters to destroy the sites. Aircraft would stay on station for up to six hours finding targets and tracking their destruction. According to Central Command, Killer Scouts increased the effectiveness of daytime strikes against the Iraqi army in Kuwait three to four times.

Radar station with wings, an E-3 of the 552nd Airborne Warning and Control Wing taxis out at Tinker AFB. Advent of AWACS has greatly enhanced tactical operations, extending the "eyes," and situational awareness, of many users of the E-3 generated "air picture." Combining long range APY-1/2 radar with on-board controllers and the 707 airframe has resulted in a platform that offers tremendous performance and flexibility. 707's range and endurance allow

AWACS to be where it's needed for the time required, while the radar's long reach allows the platform to standoff while still seeing deep into enemy territory. In addition to weapons controllers, which guide interceptors and give "heads up" to strikers on enemy aircraft locations, E-3s carry Airborne Command Elements, senior rated officers and intelligence personnel who can re-task airborne aircraft as the ebb and flow of battle demands. These ACE teams shave minutes to

hours off the reaction time required to respond to new developments in the air battle and allow friendly forces to operate at a pace that completely overwhelms the enemy - witness DESERT STORM.

Opposite, top:
E-3 leaving on a "local" training sortie - which only means it will land back at Tinker. AWACS training sorties cover the length and breadth of the country, working with Air Force, Army, Navy and Marine units nationwide. To do this, sortie lengths run 8 to

12 hours. (Right) One of fourteen Situation Display Consoles, (SDCs), on board shows typical training scenario. Multi-mode APY-1/2 radar is capable of interleaving pulse and pulse doppler signals, and these are indicated on the display by color. Yellow returns for doppler targets, blue returns for pulse targets while IFF only returns are green symbols. These are all superimposed on computer generated map. Orientation (vertical or horizontal) of open box shaped returns indicate

whether the targets are correlated to particular track symbology. Yellow "V" symbols are suspected hostile aircraft, while red inverted "V" symbols are known hostile aircraft. E-3 orbit is shown near Norfolk Va, by oval "racetrack." Red boxes are restricted areas, which in wartime could be used to identify no-fly areas (air defense free-fire zones, for example). Blue dashed and solid lines show Air Defense Identification Zone boundaries and boundaries of control areas. Each SDC can be configured to perform any surveillance or control task with overlays placed over switches to identify their

function for the task assigned that position. (The same switches do different things for different tasks) Switches to the left of the scope and under the operator's left hand control the display. Trackball under operator's right hand controls a cursor which can be used to "tag" individual returns and obtain information on the target - airspeed, heading, altitude, and, if known, identification. Switches to the right of the scope are for the complex intercom system - four different nets can be run simultaneously while also providing position to position "phone" and conference call capability.

(Below) After the sortie, the aircraft is given back to maintenance; post flight inspection and servicing can take upwards of eight hours. E-3s also carry inflight maintenance personnel, technicians to work radio, radar and display/computer problems. With the extended nature of AWACS missions and the relatively low mean time between failure of many electronics components, these technicians have saved many an AWACS sortie from early termination.

Coming off the tanker, an E-3 displays the multitude of antennas required for its 21 radios. Forward of the rotordome, the two miniature "rotordomes" are actually SATCOM antennas. These combined with 12 UHF, 3 HF, 3 VHF/AM and 1 VHF/FM allow the E-3 to put the air picture out to users ranging from theater commanders to individual fighter pilots. In addition to "voice tell" - painting the picture with words - there are also multiple data links using these radios, the most powerful of these being JTIDS which can put out in near-real time an almost exact duplicate of the SDC display.

The 57th Wing at Nellis Air Force Base, Nevada, is home to some of the most unusual, and famous, units in the Air Force. While the Weapons and Tactics Center is the host unit at Nellis, the 57th Wing owns the flying mission. This includes the Air Force Weapons School and the Combat Rescue School, the 422nd Test and Evaluation Squadron, which develops and evaluates new tactics and equipment, and the world famous Air Force demonstration squadron, the Thunderbirds. The wing is also the parent unit for the last true Wild Weasels, the 561st Fighter Squadron, and the 414th Combat Training Squadron, which runs Red Flag Exercises and owns the last Air Force Aggressor aircraft. The 549th Joint Training Squadron, which runs the Air Warrior Exercises with the Army at nearby Fort Irwin, is also part of the 57th Wing.

Above:
Two F-15E Strike Eagles from the Weapons School move into tactical formation as they enter the Nellis Range complex north of Las Vegas. Each aircraft is carrying a non-standard load of two Mk-84 2000-lb bombs and two AIM-9s.

Above:
If you don't have stealth, then you have to have Weasels. For years the venerable F-4G has been the premier aircraft in the role of supression of enemy air defenses (SEAD). In the photo above, the crew of an F-4G of the 561st Fighter Squadron tests the ALE-40 chaff and flare dispenser.

Left:
These "G-sels" are on their way to drop CBU-87 cluster munitions. Free-fall bombs such as CBUs are the armament of last resort for the Weasels with HARMs being the first choice. In situations where enemy radars don't stay up long enough to use HARMs, the preferred weapon is the Maverick. Weasels assigned to work Northern Iraq during the Gulf War had tremendous success with the Maverick, targeting sites that were not radiating as well as tanks, trucks and artillery.

Facing Page:
Two Weapons School F-16Cs in the Elgin Military Operating Area carrying non-standard loads of only two Mk-82 500-lb iron bombs.

The Weapons School is the Air Force's graduate school for pilots. The incredibly intense five and a half month-long course includes 200 to 300 hours

of academic instruction, 20 to 45 flights and a thesis. Only five percent of the elligible officers in the Air Force are selected to attend this highly specialized school.

During the course, students are taught practically everything they need to know about their aircraft, its weapons and how they are employed in combat. It is a high pressure environment where students are constantly evaluated as they learn the capabilities of, and tactics for, their specific aircraft.

Upon graduation, "target arms" (so named because alumni wear a distinctive "Graduate" patch that includes a target in the design) return to their units as weapons and tactics instructors.

Below:
The Aggressors live on in the 414th Combat Training Squadron at Nellis. Now flying Block 30 F-16Cs, the Aggressors support Red Flag, the Weapons School and various large scale exercises at Nellis.

F-15C Eagles of the
Weapons School in
"admin" formation in the
Nellis Range complex.

The Nellis Range is
probably more famous than
the base itself, with 3.5
million acres encompass-
ing the Frenchmen's Flats

Nuclear Test site, Tonopah
Test Range airfield (home
of the F-117 in its "black"
days) and Groom Lake.
Pilots call Groom Lake
either "the Box" or "Elvis'
Home," and it either does
not exist or houses UFOs
depending on who you ask.

Below:
Eagles don't just fly high. Low level tactics are still practiced not far from the Nevada desert. Without suppression of air defenses, going low is the only viable way to get to the target . . . if you are not stealthy. The low altitude regime is extremely demanding and requires frequent training to be proficient and safe. Much more time has to be spent just flying the jet, and the potential for situational awareness "jumping into the map case" is much higher.

Likewise, the tendency to get wrapped up in tactical chores (checking six, looking in the radar, analyzing RHAW) can cause the pilot to forget priority number one – staying out of the rocks. Yanking and banking down low is just as common as it is up high. However, low level maneuvering tends to be more enthusiastic than similar maneuvers done at altitude! During ridge crossings, for example, the jet goes inverted as it passes over the top of the ridge, as the pilot aggressively pulls down to avoid zooming up into radar coverage. When the pilot doesn't pull down expeditiously, it's referred to as the "Ivan thanks you very much" maneuver.

Above:

With number three maneu-
vering to fall back into trail
formation, these Weapons
School A-10s are carrying
the standard Warthog training load of an Infra-red and
a TV Maverick and a cap-
tive AIM-9 Sidewinder.

The A-10s are shown
entering the "Sally
Corridor", the main route
from Nellis into Range airspace from the Southeast.
From here flights will enter
the Elgin MOA for air-to-
air work or go up to "Texas
Lake" (the dry lake bed
resembling the state of
Texas) to enter the rest of
the range complex. "Blue"
strike packages flying Red
Flag exercises normally
follow the Sally Corridor
route.

Joint STARS...

A revolutionary capability for Air Combat Command, proven in Desert Storm.

The **Joint Surveillance Target Attack Radar System** possesses an unprecedented combination of capabilities – providing commanders with greatly enhanced situational awareness.

Joint STARS revolutionizes peace keeping – detects and exposes preparations for aggression and warfighting – multiplies the effectiveness of air and surface forces.

For more information contact
Surveillance & Battle Management Systems-Melbourne, P.O. Box 9650, Melbourne, FL 32902-9650

NORTHROP GRUMMAN

Pre-production E-8C over the Atlantic during a test sortie. This real-time, man-in-the-loop system promises to revolutionize warfare by giving commanders an unprecedented view of the battlefield and allowing ground and air attacks to be directed at an enemy that can not hide. One of the most crucial tenets of warfare is being taken away from the enemy - the element of surprise.

Advancements in radar technology now allow an airborne platform to stand-off from the battlefield and "see" the enemy's every move in any weather. The Army and Air Force are jointly developing the Joint Surveillance Target Attack Radar System, or Joint STARS to exploit this technology. The system uses Boeing 707s housing the radar and its displays with a distributed network of ground stations receiving the radar "picture" via data link. The radome is mounted on the lower forward fuselage (pg 219) with the radar and computer equipment housed in the former baggage areas and the 17 display consoles in what used to be the passenger compartment. The radar operates in two modes: a moving target indicator (MTI) mode that shows all moving vehicles across hundreds of miles and a synthetic aperture radar (SAR) mode that produces a near photographic radar "picture" of stationary objects in a small area.

During DESERT STORM the two E-8 test aircraft and five prototype ground stations were deployed despite the fact they were still in the midst of development and testing - seven years prior to the planned initial operational capability. In 30 days a unique team of Air Combat Command, Material Command, Army and Contractor personnel had the 4411th Joint STARS Sq. (Provisional) ready for deployment and combat operations. The squadron was assigned to Riyadh, Saudi Arabia with the GSMs being further deployed at the various headquarters throughout Saudi Arabia. They flew their first sortie in theatre January 11th and immediately started developing high quality, time sensitive data. On the very first sortie, forces were observed moving from Kuwait into Saudi Arabia. At first, this was believed to be a precursor of an Iraqi preemptive attack, however it turned out to be starving

(Northrop Grumman photo)

Iraqi soldiers begging food and water from Saudi Army troops. A SAR of this can be seen on the photo below with individual Iraqi vehicles clearly visible on the road (unla-

beled arrow).

The squadron's first combat mission was flown on the night of 17 January and it flew every night after that until after the war was over. Every single tasking was filled - 52 sorties - an unbelievable accomplishment for an experimental system mounted in two 20 year old airplanes.

While the airborne part of the squadron was producing first class reconnaissance products, the GSMs were allowing ground commanders an unprecedented real-time view of the battlefield. For example, during the battle of Kafji, Marine commanders, unlike CNN, knew exactly what they were facing - an Iraqi probe and not an all out assault. Also during this battle, Joint STARS detected reinforcements departing staging areas south of Kuwait City, moving south to join the battle. At the time, there were no fighters assigned directly to Joint STARS so the convoy's location was passed to ABCCC which diverted A-10s and an AC-130 gunship to "service" the target. Eighty vehicles in the column were destroyed and it never left Kuwait.

Results such as this got the Iraqis' attention and their ground units almost ceased sending out large convoys, moving instead in small groups over short distances at a time. Joint STARS then used the SAR mode to detect stationary Iraqi vehicles and vectored fighters in to attack them. By "shooting" multiple SARs around a central point, even large, multiple unit Iraqi formations could be accurately plotted - and attacked. Every night during the air war, F-15Es, LANTIRN F-16s and Pave Tack equipped F-111Es were directed to targets with excellent results - for the Allies.

In addition to giving ground commanders and their staffs a unique view of the war, the GSMs were also used for targeting. For example, the GSM at CENTAF headquarters was often used for providing targets to aircraft that had "lost" their primary target due to weather or other factors. One night the Army specialist who was man-

(Northrop Grumman photo)

the MTI frame, below.

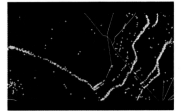

Each yellow cross is an individual moving vehicle, the white lines are roads from the computer generated map overlaid on the radar data. This shows the Marine advance into Southern Kuwait (two right columns moving Northeast) with a column of allied troops (somewhat disoriented) advancing basically eastward. Marines in the advance detected the approaching (allied) column and were preparing to engage what they thought was a flanking attack, when they were notified by their headquarters that their intended targets were friendlies, a situation they had seen developing on the Joint STARS ground station. The allied unit was made aware of their navigation error shortly before this frame was made and their 90 degree turn is clearly visible.

CENTAF Commander, Gen. Horner walked in and asked if there were any targets suitable for B-52s. The young man showed the General where a large concentration of vehicles had been discovered earlier. General Horner got the coordinates of the concentration and the target was struck by B-52s shortly afterward leaving the specialist nearly as shocked as the Iraqis.

When the ground war started, the Moving Target Indicator mode of the radar became Joint STARS' primary tool. Now fighters would be directed to moving targets - and be given position updates on those targets until they were almost overhead. The best example of how effective a real-time, man-in-the-loop system can be was during the Iraqi retreat from Kuwait. All the bridges across the lower Euphrates had been cut, but surveillance officers on Joint STARS saw MTI tracks crossing the river - a pontoon bridge had been thrown across the river and was allowing Iraqi units to

escape. Based on the Joint STARS data, fighters with laser guided bombs were diverted to destroy the bridge. Then, using the SAR mode, the E-8 crew saw that the Iraqis had been unable to stop the flow of units moving towards the now destroyed bridge and a huge concentration of vehicles was piling up in the ensuing traffic snarl. Joint STARS diverted fighters with cluster bombs to the area; with catastrophic results for the Iraqis.

Another use of Joint STARS data can be seen in

With the end of the war, Joint STARS was quickly redeployed to the States to avoid any further impact on its development schedule. Today both E-8s that were in the war are part of a contingency force that is ready to duplicate Joint STARS DESERT STORM success until the production system is declared mission ready in 1997.

Walt Bylciw, Vice President, F 119 Programs, Pratt & Whitney

"BASICALLY, THIS IS WHAT IS MEANT BY GOOD OL' AMERICAN KNOW HOW."

If evidence is needed that the American spirit of innovation is alive and well, the F-22 fighter is the ultimate proof. It will keep America the leader in world aviation, supplying vast new technologies to other industries at the same time. The F-22 Integrated Product Development concept alone serves as the model for the aircraft and engine industry. And its cost effectiveness will set the standard, costing 30% less to maintain, support and deploy than current fighters. F-22. Not only will it represent America in the decades to come. It will represent America at its best.

F-22
LOCKHEED · BOEING
PRATT & WHITNEY

nition. For air-to-ground missions, the F-22 can carry two GBU-29 JDAM 1000 lb bombs displacing four of the AMRAAMs. An advanced fly-by-wire flight control system combined with thrust vectoring of the engines makes the F-22 the worlds most agile fighter. Sustained high G maneuvering is possible with no limits on angle of attack. Sixty degrees or greater AOA can be achieved with complete controllability - the nose always goes where the pilot wants it. With this kind of capability the F-22 can fly rings around anything - including "cobra maneuvering" Su-27/35 Flankers.

F-22 cockpit (below and on page 223) allows the pilot tremendous visibility and "situational awareness approaching omniscience." The cockpit has no "steam gauges." For the first time in a fighter there are no instruments, the HUD is the primary flight reference with back-up heads-down CRT displays (small displays left and right of up-

The future of Air Combat Command - an F-22 on the ramp at the Lockheed Martin factory, Marietta, Georgia. The F-22 features increased range, speed, maneuverability and survivability. It is by every measure superior to the F-15 it will replace, starting in 2004.

Two 35,000 lb + thrust F119 engines push the F-22 to supersonic speeds without the use of fuel hungry afterburners. This supercruise capability imparts a significant tactical advantage while greatly expanding the area a flight of fighters can patrol. Stealth requirements demand that all weapons

and fuel be carried internally, but for deployments four 600 gal tanks can be mounted under the wings. The jet can carry six AIM-120Cs, two AIM-9s and has an internal 20mm M61 rotary cannon with 480 rounds of ammu-

front control keyboard). Large color LCD multi-function displays show defensive information (left), attack information (right), systems status (lower center) and "big picture" (upper center). To "build" these displays, processors combine information from a variety of on and off-board sensors and require an unbelievable amount of computational power. The F-22's two common integrated processors have a combined throughput equal to that of four Cray supercomputers. Note that the defensive display shows the range of ground based SAMs, while the center and right displays have expanded tabular information on the designated target and the wingman in the lower corners of the displays. The wingman's fuel, weapons status and targeting data are passed via an inflight data link. The radar has three modes: full up, low probability of intercept, and a stealth "sniff" mode. Off-board sensors become very important in the last

Photo by John Rossino

two modes. The pilot flies the aircraft with an F-16 style side-stick controller, that, unlike the Viper's, does move.

The most frequently asked question about the F-22 is, "why do we need this jet?" It's easy to think we might not, if you didn't have a real good feel for the potential threat. The SA-10 and SA-12 SAM systems and the Su-27/35 Flanker with its AA-10 and 11 missiles all present an overwhelming threat to the F-15. Even without these systems, Iraq was able to fashion an air defense system over Baghdad that the F-15 was not allowed to fly into. With the breakup of the Soviet Union, advanced systems are widely available, much more so than

during the Cold War. It's not too difficult to imagine a replay of the Gulf War, ten years from now, with Iraq having the advanced systems listed above. Without the F-22, F-117s would have to work with SEAD F-16s to hunt down and kill SAM sites, since the SA-10 and 12 both have longer range than the HARM missile. Since both of these SAMs are mobile, this would not be a simple task. Then, after holes are knocked in the SAM belts the F-15 would be up against an adversary that has a "bigger stick" - the AA-10 armed Su-27/35s would be shooting at F-15s before the F-15s were in range of the Flankers. The chances of repeating the near-zero loss

rates of the '91 war are slim. But with the F-22, significant holes open in the SAM belts due to the reduced range caused by the F-22's low radar cross section. Once past the SAMs, the tables are turned, with the F-22 enjoying the advantage of being able to fire first without being targeted in return. A repeat of our earlier success seems much more likely. Combined with the fact that a wing of F-22s uses half the scarce airlift required by a wing of F-15s to get to the fight, and once there requires half the number of maintainers to keep up and running, the F-22 makes a lot of sense.

Acknowledgments

The problem with acknowledgments is that, no matter how careful you are, someone always gets left out, To whoever that someone is who should have been listed below, our sincere apologies. There are so many people who helped make this book happen that any attempt to recognize them will surely come up short. Having said that . . .

First and foremost thanks go to General Mike Loh, who approved the concept of an ACC chapter to the Real Heroes series when it was simply a gleam in authors' eyes. Despite knowing the impact this effort would have on his operators and maintainers, he wholeheartedly supported this book even as he worked to combine former TAC, SAC and MAC units into ACC.

For taking General Loh's approval and turning it into opportunities to visit bases and fly with units, thanks go to Lieutenant General Lawrence E. Boese and Major General Lee A. Downer and their staff as well as Colonels Michael Gallagher and Don Black and their troops in Public Affairs.

At the unit level, multitudes of folks worked hard to get us where we needed to be, to make photo opportunities happen and make us smart on what ACC people do and how they do it. Additionally, thanks go to all of those who shared their ideas with us, making Real Heroes, Air Combat Command better than it would have otherwise been. In particular thanks to Major General William S. Hinton, Jr., Major General David J. McCloud, Brigadier General Gregory Martin, Brigadier General Ronald Marcotte, Brigadier General Ralph Pasini, Brigadier General John Rutledge, and Brigadier General James L. Sandstrom. With "all-star" help like this, how could we possibly fail?

Colonel Mike Decuir, Colonel Michael A. Kenny, Colonel Gregory Power, Colonel Ron Hindmarsh, Colonel Steve Schmidt; Lieutenant Colonels John Bellanger, Anthony Imondi, Don Ross and Keith Wagner; Majors Ralph Merz, Steve Seroka and Earl Shellner; Captain Matt Gruner, Captain Bill Harrison, Captain "Sticks" Martin, Captain Bob Russell, Captain Larry Wildasin; First Lieutenant Pat Hudson and First Lieutenant Johanna Kelly; Master Sergeants Ed Drohan and John Johnson; Technical Sergeant Don Lottes; Staff Sergeants Deborah Clayton and Gary Padrta; Senior Airman Deborah VanNierop and Mr. Steve Pivnick and Mr. Jeff Rhodes all went "above and beyond" in making things happen. Thanks to each and every one of you for your extra effort - you can never understand how much we appreciate your professionalism and dedication.

A special thanks to all the life support troops, maintainers and aircrews who endured photo flights, before, during and after. Flying photo chase is NOT fun - it's hard work. Thanks for always putting Randy where he needed to be to get the best photos possible. Fair winds, clear skies....and good hunting, guys.

Finally, Dave would like to say thanks to Randy for letting one each slightly used fighter pilot be a part of this effort and Randy, as always, thanks, Andrea for her limitless patience and understanding.